Buddhist Psychotherapy

Hyunsoo Jeon

Buddhist Psychotherapy

Wisdom from Early Buddhist Teaching

Springer

Hyunsoo Jeon
Hyunsoo Jeon's Psychiatry Clinic
Seoul, Korea (Republic of)

ISBN 978-3-030-63097-3 ISBN 978-3-030-63098-0 (eBook)
https://doi.org/10.1007/978-3-030-63098-0

This Springer imprint is published by the registered company Springer Nature Switzerland AG
The registered company address is: Gewerbestrasse 11, 6330 Cham, Switzerland

Preface

People see Freud's psychoanalysis which emerged in the early 1900s as the beginning of scientific psychotherapy. But I say with confidence that the first scientific psychotherapy is Buddhism, founded by the Buddha 2600 years ago. Buddhism is in itself a complete psychotherapy. Only people are not very aware of this. Through observation, the Buddha fully understood what kind of beings humans are. Based on this observation, he found a complete solution to the various forms of suffering that humans endure, and set forth a specific method for this. Whoever fully follows the path that the Buddha set forth is able to be completely free from suffering. The Buddha's disciples saw that the Buddha's teachings would be extremely important for people in the future. And so they passed on those teachings orally for the first 600 or so years, and afterwards recorded it in writing. The three baskets (Tipiṭaka) of discourses (Sutta), discipline (Vinaya), and special doctrines (Abhidhamma) are the textbooks of Buddhist psychotherapy.

It took over 30 years for me to reach this realization. It began with a meeting with Professor Ko Ikjin. When I heard Professor Ko explain the doctrine of karma in 1985, the thought that "Buddhism is the truth" came to my mind. I directly applied the professor's teaching of the doctrine of karma in my life and thanks to that teaching was able to live much more comfortably. So if people with mental illnesses understand and apply Buddhism in their lives, it seemed that it would help them greatly, as it did for me. I thought psychotherapy and Buddhism could be connected. Afterwards, I walked the two paths of Buddhism and psychotherapy for a long time.

Sometimes I struggled, unable to see ahead. The 15 years I studied and practiced Buddhism from the time that Professor Ko passed away in 1988 to when I realized the properties of the body and mind through meditation in Myanmar in 2003 were quite difficult. But fortunately during that time, I was able to meet Professor Rhee Dongshick and learn psychotherapy. I studied for 12 years at the Korean Academy of Psychotherapists, led by Professor Rhee who had created Tao-(道)psychotherapy, and as I performed psychotherapy at my clinic, I formed my own view on the subject.

From 2000 I again took time to advance my study and practice of Buddhism. In 2003, I formed a study group of Buddhism and psychotherapy. There, psychiatrists, psychologists, monks, and Buddhist practitioners put their heads together to study these two fields, and together we founded the Korean Association of Buddhism and Psychotherapy in 2007. My colleagues and I did a lot of research and thought a lot about how these two fields could be connected. This was very helpful in establishing the system of Buddhist psychotherapy.

In November 2013, I closed my clinic doors for a second time to concentrate on meditation and was able to successfully practice Samatha and Vipassanā meditation. And as my doubts about Buddhism completely went away, I was able to join the two paths I had walked during that time as one. In fall of 2014, my practice of Samatha and Vipassanā came to an end and I was able to establish my own system of Buddhist psychotherapy. This is my long journey of establishing the system of Buddhist psychotherapy and introducing it to the world.

The next year, I lectured for 3 days at a training course for monks of the Jogye order in Korea on why Buddhism was psychotherapy and how one could treat mental illness with Buddhism. Hearing about this, Professor Kim Jaesung who had worked with me for a long time at the Korean Association of Buddhism and Psychotherapy suggested a Buddhist psychotherapy workshop. And so I ran a workshop at Beoblyeonsa temple next to Gyeongbokgung for 3 h once a month from March to December, 2016, for a total of ten sessions. A diverse range of about 80 people including psychiatrists and Buddhist practitioners attended the workshop. In the process of preparing for the workshop, as I lectured in front of people, and as I received feedback from the participants, Buddhist psychotherapy began to take shape.

Each session of the workshop was recorded through video and audio. Its contents were then transcribed by one of the workshop participants, Yim Mijeong. I extend my gratitude to Yim Mijeong who undertook this immense task with pleasure, saying that it helped her own practice. It was thanks to her that I was able to write this book. Lee Giseon, the editor of Bulgwang Publications also participated in the workshop. He expressed his desire to help in the publication as well as study Buddhist psychotherapy. The conversations we shared about the book late at night after the workshop were greatly helpful.

Now one stone has been set in the great journey of Buddhist psychotherapy. There are still many things to be done. It may be difficult for people without experience in meditation to understand the truth that I know through meditation. Helping them understand is the task that has been laid out in front of me. For example, my task is to reveal and help people understand the mechanisms of unwholesome consciousnesses that cause mental illnesses to arise, and the mechanisms of wholesome consciousnesses that help the mind recover. Only then can Buddhist psychotherapy be a scientific psychology, a scientific psychotherapy.

Many people have provided help in coming to this point. Above all the help of my wife has been a great support. It is not an exaggeration to say that my path to Buddhism began with meeting my wife. I extend my gratitude to my wife. Meeting her gave me the opportunity to open my eyes anew to Buddhism and making me who I am today. I am especially thankful for her understanding and belief in me through the many times I was not home in order to practice meditation and my being constantly busy with work even when I was at home. I do not know how to repay her. I am also thankful for the patients who participated in establishing the new path of Buddhist psychotherapy. It was thanks to their participation that I was able to concretely understand how Buddhism helps in real life. And without my colleagues who walked the path of Buddhism and psychotherapy together and who provided mutual support, my method of Buddhist psychotherapy would not be possible today. I extend my gratitude to all of the people who mutually helped polish the two fields of Buddhism and psychotherapy during this time.

In this book, there are also contents that are in my previous books. Despite the contents being the same, I have approached them with the new perspective of Buddhist psychotherapy and have tried to supplement them.

I am happy and honored to be able to contribute this small part to such a noble task. I am confident that Buddhist psychotherapy will play a big role in effectively treating people's mental illnesses and suffering in the future.

Seoul, Korea (Republic of) Hyunsoo Jeon
Autumn 2020

Endorsement

This is a unique offering by a trained Korean psychiatrist steeped in early Buddhist psychology and meditation practice. Dr. Hyunsoo Jeon learned Pali and Sanskrit, the language of the original Buddhist scriptures, and spent 30 years contemplating the teachings and stories of the Buddha in light of his psychodynamically informed work with patients. This book especially speaks to those who are familiar with and inclined towards Buddhist concepts and practice. Readers will come away with an appreciation of early Buddhist psychology as a wisdom tradition with profound insight into human suffering and how to alleviate it. Dr. Jeon understands many of these insights from direct, meditative experience and he invites his readers to do the same.

Christopher Germer, PhD
Lecturer on Psychiatry (Part-time), Harvard Medical School
Co-editor, *Mindfulness and Psychotherapy*

Contents

About the Author

Hyunsoo Jeon Born 1956 in Pusan in Korea he became a psychiatrist and psychotherapy specialist after graduating from Busan National University School of Medicine and receiving neuropsychiatry training at the Soonchunhyang University Hospital. He attended Hanyang University Medical School where he obtained his master' and doctoral degrees. He was introduced to Buddhist teachings 2 years after becoming a neuropsychiatry resident. After that, he met with patients and studied Buddhism concurrently, using Buddhist wisdom to aid him in treating his patients. The use of Buddhist wisdom was so effective that he detailed his experiences in his books.

In 1990, he opened Hyunsoo Jeon Psychiatry Clinic. In 2003, he took a month off from his clinic to go to Burma to partake in Vipassanā training. Later that year, he gathered specialists in Buddhism, psychology, and psychiatry to study together and hold discussions, This gathering developed into the Korean Association of Buddhism and Psychotherapy in 2007. In March 2009, he took a year off from therapy to practice Buddhism, travel, and write books. In March 2010, he reopened his clinic and returned to helping patients. He also spent 2 years practicing Samatha and Vipassanā at Myanmar and Korea.

He has authored the following books in Koran and English: *Cry When You Want to Cry and A Psychiatrist's Wisdom from the Buddha: Stories of Healing the Mind*, *A Psychiatrist's "Guidebook for the Mind,"* collaborated in writing *Value of Labor: A Buddhist* Perspective, 32 Lectures on Early Buddhism given by a psychiatrist, collaborated in writing Lessons on the Buddha's Emotions (all in Korean), and *Samatha, Jhana, and Vipassana* (in English, published in Wisdom Publications in America) as well as translating Mark Epstein's book *Thoughts Without a Thinker* into Korean.

He was awarded "Grand Prize of Wonhyo Scholarship" from Korean Buddhist Institute in 2018.

He presented "No self based psychotherapy," in 63rd Annual meeting of The American Academy of Psychodynamic Psychiatry and Psychoanalysis in May 2019.

About the Translator

Hanul Jun graduated with a Master of Arts in Asian Languages and Cultures from the University of Michigan in 2017, where his primary focus was on Buddhist meditation practice. He met Dr. Jeon in 2013 and worked with him on a number of translation projects, including *Samatha, Jhana, and Vipassana Practice at the Pa-Auk Monastery: A Meditator's Experience*, published by Wisdom Publications in 2018.

Hanul has been practicing mindfulness meditation for nearly 20 years and ordained as a monk in Myanmar for 3 months in 2013. Throughout the years, Hanul has traveled to many countries to learn about the different traditions of mediation, including Korean Seon meditation (Zen), Tibetan meditation, and Theravada Vipassanā meditation. He has taught meditation at various youth camps in both the United States and in Korea.

Currently, Hanul is a Policy Specialist at Google in Austin Texas, where he continues to lead weekly guided mindfulness meditation sessions at the office.

Chapter 1
What Is Buddhist Psychotherapy?

If we had to pick out a founder of Buddhist psychotherapy, I would say that it was the Buddha. Based on a complete understanding of humans and the world, the Buddha proposed a personalized method to escape from suffering to each person who sought him out, and those who put his teachings into practice were all liberated from suffering. Seeing this occur again and again in the Nikāyas (Buddhist scriptures), I became convinced that Buddhism was an excellent psychotherapy, not to be outdone by any other psychotherapy.

The First Act of Buddhist Psychotherapy

My biggest question I had was, "Would Buddhist psychotherapy be possible, like Freud's psychoanalysis or Jung's analytical psychology?" It took me 30 years to come up with an answer to this question. I will briefly talk about the journey of finding this answer, as it may help people understand Buddhist psychotherapy.

It started in 1985. That was the year I met my first teacher. When I first met him in his office, he was in his early 50s and I was 30. When he asked about what I was doing, I told him that I was a second-year resident doctor majoring in psychiatry. Then, he told me, "Buddhism is the perfect system for resolving the suffering of human beings. And wouldn't the psychiatry that you're studying right now ultimately be resolving people's mental illnesses? In my opinion, if we just change the terms of Buddhism into a system of treating mental illness, it will become an excellent psychiatric system." I thought, "He seems like an incredible person. I should learn more from him." Then in November, I began attending the study sessions he was running and started to learn about Buddhism.

This person was Professor Ko Ikjin. While he was attending medical school at Jeonnam University in his 20s, he became infected with a disease that caused his heart to be filled with water. Since his heart was filled with water, it was not able to

H. Jeon, *Buddhist Psychotherapy*, https://doi.org/10.1007/978-3-030-63098-0_1

beat frequently enough. And so edemas formed all over his body, making it so that he could not walk and could only lie down. Though he recovered to some degree after spending several years in the hospital, his condition was still serious, and he convalesced at a temple that belonged to his mother. Then one day, his eyes became fixed upon the following words within the Heart Sutra which was hanging on a frame, "no eyes, ears, nose, tongue, body, and mind" (無眼耳鼻舌身意). He told me that he thought, "I have eyes, but why did the Buddha say there are no eyes?" After thinking about this again and again for 3 years, he came to his own realization, "Ah! This is the reason why the Buddha said there are no eyes."

In December 1985, the year that I attended the professor's study group, something happened that changed my life. It was that I heard from the professor about the way the world works. The professor called this "the doctrine of karma." He talked about how the world is formed and the way it works based on the doctrine of karma. As I listened to his explanation, it felt like my eyes were opened. I thought, "Buddhism is the truth. This is something I should practice my whole life."

That year, I was terribly busy as a second-year medical resident doctor. I was of course very stressed in a culture of vertical decision-making within the world of medicine. On top of that, I also got married that year, and it was not easy to maintain a work-life balance. But after learning about the doctrine of karma from Professor Ko and applying its logic in my own life, things got much easier. And so I thought, "This logic would be helpful for people struggling with mental illness." It is here that my ideas for Buddhist psychotherapy began.

I first thought of using Buddhism in psychotherapy. This would mean leaving psychotherapy as it is and adding in some of the principles of karma. I actually tried doing this during my time as a medical officer in the army, and people understood and accepted it well.

The Buddhism that Professor Ko taught me was kind of unique. It was different from other kinds of Buddhism that exist today in terms of its interpretation. And so I asked Professor Ko where he got his teachings from. He replied that the teachings were in the "Nikāyas," scriptures of Early Buddhism. And so I made up my mind to learn Pali and study the Nikāyas. This decision played a significant role in helping me establish Buddhist psychotherapy.

There was someone else aside from Professor Ko who was very influential to me. It was Professor Rhee Dongshick. I first met Professor Rhee at a seminar on the topic of the meeting between psychiatrists and Buddhist practitioners at Seogang University in 1984. I still remember that seminar today because it was then that I first found out that there was a way to bring together Buddhism and psychotherapy. I received training analysis from Professor Rhee for 4 years and 2 months from November 1988 to December 1992. Afterwards I came to realize, "Ah, this is what a person's mind is!" Before that, I had been making diagnoses and prescribing medicine as a psychiatrist, but I did not really know why people became ill. But after receiving training analysis from Professor Rhee, I was able to know more definitively in my own way why mental illnesses arise.

To become a psychotherapist, everyone must go through three steps.

The first step is undergoing our own training analysis. Through this training analysis, we resolve our own mental problems. I still vividly remember the time when I first sought out Professor Rhee and he asked me "What are your mental problems?" There is another goal to receiving training analysis, namely to experience the treatment process. It is knowing first-hand what a patient experiences while undergoing treatment. On the basis of this experience, we are later able to know how a patient we are treating feels. The most important thing that is obtained through training analysis is the ability to see ourselves objectively. It is being able to see ourselves as others see us. Normally, we do not see ourselves as we are very well. We see ourselves through our thoughts. Are not there things we see so obviously when we look at others? Likewise, there are things that others see clearly when they look at us but that we ourselves are not able to notice at all. For you see, in the process of training analysis, we are continuously questioned as to why we think the way we do. By being questioned like this, we are able to see ourselves.

The second step is case supervision. This means recording or transcribing the treatment cases we have worked on and receiving feedback on them from an experienced therapist. There are two goals to this. First, problems that we have not yet resolved may surface from these recorded treatments. These are what we receive guidance on. Second, we learn from the vast experiences of an experienced therapist. Case supervision can be done individually and in a group.

The third step is attending theoretical seminars. What is important to note here is the fact that there was originally no such thing as a theory. Instead, there is only reality. For example, if Freud only wanted to exchange ideas with a few people close to him, he could have just talked about his ideas. But 'didn't he set up a system and write because he wanted to share his views with people from other countries, or even people from a different era.' We call this theory, but when attending theoretical seminars, we must be able to see the experiences within the theories. We must learn the experiences. We must learn the experiences of our predecessor therapists.

Professor Ko passed away in 1988. Twelve years later, so until around the year 2000, I established my foundation by undergoing training analysis, case supervision, and attending theoretical seminars. While I presented on the treatment cases I had worked on, I accumulated many experiences on the side of psychotherapy.

The Second Act of Buddhist Psychotherapy

Then in 2002, I stumbled upon a certain book. It was called *In this Very Life*. Among the famous teachers in Myanmar, there is the Mahasi Sayadaw, and his top disciple was Sayadaw U Pandita. *In this Very Life* is the book that summarizes the talks that Sayadaw U Pandita gave when he held a 3-month retreat for Western practitioners at the Insight Meditation Society (IMS) in the United States.

Before I read this book, I kind of looked down on vipassanā meditation. I had thought, "How could one master the teachings of Buddhism by just observing the body and mind, when Buddhism is extremely deep and profound." But the book states that by observing the body and mind moment to moment, we are able to perceive the three marks of existence, namely impermanence (*anicca*), suffering (*dukkha*), and no-self (*anatta*).

Let us briefly address the three marks of existence here. Impermanence (*anicca*) does not have the connotations of words like "worthless" or "futile" that we use in our daily lives, but rather means that "everything changes." The fact that everything continuously changes moment to moment is suffering (*dukkha*). This is a teaching that is difficult to understand. However, when we look at it fundamentally, change is suffering. Things change, which is suffering, but we are not able to control any of this. We as humans are made up of the body and mind, but when we look closely, we don't have any control over the body or the mind. This is no-self (*anatta*). No-self does not mean that "there is no me," but rather it means that there is nothing we can control within our body and mind. Because we are not able to control the body and mind, we have no choice but to endure everything that arises in them. We are beings that have to undergo every experience in our lives, pleasant or unpleasant.

Based on the suttas and commentaries, Sayadaw U Pandita clearly explains that we can know the three marks of experience by observing the body and mind moment to moment. After discovering this, my perception towards vipassanā changed. With this change in perception, I started to read many books on vipassanā and went around asking people near me what I would have to do to practice vipassanā meditation. Many people told me to go to Myanmar. When I asked how I should practice in Myanmar, they told me to shave my head and become a monk.

So in July, 2003 I went to Myanmar. I went to the Chanmyay Meditation Center in Yangon, shaved my head, and became a monk (*bhikkhu*). There I observed the body and mind from the moment I opened my eyes in the morning to the time I went to sleep at night. At the meditation hall, we practice both sitting and walking meditation, observing as they were the phenomena that arose. Walking meditation always lasted an hour, while sitting meditation was for as long as possible. When sitting, we were allowed to straighten our backs, but we were not allowed to change our posture by moving our legs. For example, if our legs went numb, we would first just observe them. And if it became unbearable, we would get up. After getting up, we would practice walking meditation for an hour. When practicing walking meditation, we observed phenomena arising as they are. And after we finished walking, we would practice sitting meditation again. In the meditation hall, we would alternate between sitting and walking meditation. Outside the meditation hall, we would practice what is called observing daily activities, where we would do things slowly while observing all the phenomena that arose.

When I arrived at the Chanmyay Meditation Center, I first thought, "Up to this point, I feel like I have already been observing the body and mind to some degree, so why do I have to do this?" And so I asked Sayadaw U Sobhita, my teacher, this question every day. "Why do I have to do this?" And he replied, "To know!" A week later, I started to feel pain while practicing sitting meditation, but it seemed like I was feeling each individual cell. Something was arising from each of these cells, and contrary to what I had thought about the body in the past, I came to know that though the body belongs to me, it is its own vast world that is completely separate from me. I experienced in my own way, "Ah, this is no-self!"

After learning that we practiced observation to have these kinds of experiences, I stopped asking. Afterwards I experienced many things and realized impermanence, suffering, and no-self in my own way. I also began to have a deeper understanding of psychotherapy. I started to realize, "The mind has these kinds of properties." "I can see why a patient is ill." "I could do these things to cure their illness."

Later, on my way back to Korea, I came to meet Sayadaw U Tejaniya at the Shwe Oo Min Meditation Center for around an hour through an arrangement of a monk that I knew. The Shwe Oo Min Meditation Center is famous for its practice of observing the mind. Though Sayadaw U Tejaniya was rather young, he was the main teacher of the meditation center. I asked him a few questions. I will share one of them as it is important in terms of psychotherapy.

I asked Sayadaw U Tejaniya, "In the process of treating a patient as a psychiatrist, patients are able to gain insight into their own problems, but they keep repeating their past problems. Why does this happen, and how can I resolve this?" Sayadaw U Tejaniya responded, "Help the patient see it for themselves." Hearing this and thinking about it, I realized that in the field of therapy, we did not focus on treating the patient by helping them see things for themselves. In fact, is not it the case that a patient spends only 1 or 2 h a week with the therapist and the rest of the time with themselves? So, it is extremely important that the patient be someone who is able to take care of themselves well in that time. This is exactly what people who perform psychotherapy must help their patients with. Sayadaw U Tejaniya's words were extremely helpful to me.

When I realized that knowing the properties of the body and mind by observing them in this way was a huge help to treating patients, I was able to begin my second journey of Buddhist Psychotherapy. After Professor Ko passed away, I had lost myself in studying Buddhism. But in order to read Buddhist scriptures in their original language, I first studied Sanskrit for about a year and a half, and then studied Pali. I then held meetings where I read the early scriptures (Nikāyas) in Pali with Professors of Buddhist Studies. Along the way, I went to Myanmar, and realized that observing the body and mind was extremely beneficial. Then I had this thought, "I have lost myself in studying Buddhism and practicing meditation. This is the only one thing left for me to do." From then until now I have constantly observed the body and mind. If thoughts arose, I would stop myself and return to the present. And I have followed the five precepts of a lay Buddhist, namely not to kill, not to steal, not to engage in sexual misconduct, not to lie, not to consume intoxicating substances such as alcohol.

From July 2003, I continued to observe the body and mind in this way. During that time, I realized a lot of things in my own way and did not have much doubt.

Though I did not have much doubt, for a period of 2 years from 2007 to 2008 I did not do anything except to see my patients and focus on reading the four main Nikāyas. My goal was to figure out what the Buddha's main teachings were, what among them I experienced and what I did not, and to determine whether or not Buddhism could really be a psychology or psychotherapy.

Reading the Nikāyas I was able to know clearly—that the foundation of the Buddha's teachings was the law of cause and effect, and through this cause and effect we are beings that, despite being no-self, have no choice but to continue to be reborn in samsāra (the circle of existence). Escaping from the suffering of samsāra is the essence of the Buddha's teachings. All the methods of meditation in Buddhism are aimed at the goal of understanding these teachings and putting them into practice. I was able to understand many of them by observing the body and mind. But I was unable to experience two very important things in Buddhism. One was the state of jhāna (absorption), and the other was the true nature or process of samsāra. And so I came to another resolution, "Now I need to cultivate jhāna and afterwards see the truth of samsāra, namely how each one of our rebirths is connected with each other."

While looking for a way to do this, I learned that this was possible at the Pa Auk Forest Meditation Center in Myanmar. Hearing that 2 years would be enough time to cultivate jhāna and practice Pa Auk meditation, I made plans to take off about 2 years from my clinic. This time I was not able to go to Myanmar, so I practiced Samatha meditation for 6 months in Malaysia and Korea. Afterwards I decided that Samatha meditation was not for me, and I opened my clinic again. When I returned, I finished reading the parts of the Nikāyas I was not able to get to before.

After reading almost all of the Nikāyas, I stumbled upon by chance a special experience[1] during my practice. After this experience, I wanted to once again attempt to practice meditation. And so, in November 2013 I closed my clinic again and this time succeeded in my attempt to practice Samatha meditation. When you cultivate absorption, the eye of wisdom opens. When the eye of wisdom opens, you are able to see ultimate materiality and mentality that is invisible to the naked eye.

The Essence of Psychotherapy

Before we go into the details of Buddhist psychotherapy, I think it is necessary to look into what psychotherapy is. There are many of different kinds of psychotherapy. When I looked at a summary of psychotherapy on Wikipedia in early 2016, I found over 1000 different kinds of psychotherapy.

There is a framework for understanding people in every psychotherapy. This means seeing, "people are such-and-such beings." These frameworks for understanding people are the results of observations and experiences of each person who

[1] For more information, see pp. 5–6 of Jeon [1].

created a school of psychotherapy. For example, by analyzing his own dreams, Freud became convinced in the possibility of psychoanalysis. Professor Rhee Dongshick, the creator of "Tao-(道)psychotherapy," saw that there was a nuclear emotion in a person's every action and emphasizes understanding them. Each and every psychotherapy possesses such frameworks and works to resolve a patients' problems through the work of treatment within the relationship between the therapist and the patient. There is no psychotherapy that escapes this. Therefore, the essence of psychotherapy is resolving the problems of a mental health patient through deep conversations, accompanied by the framework of seeing the life or problems of an individual person and by extension humanity. In this process, the mental health patient needs to feel that the therapist understands them and needs to receive practical help in solving their problems. Therefore, a therapist must be able to have a good relationship with the mental health patient and must be able to understand others well. These are the basic components of psychotherapy.

The main psychotherapies are Freud's psychoanalysis, Jung's analytical psychology, Adler's individual psychology, Carl Rogers' client-centered therapy (or person-centered therapy). Among these we will look into Carl Rogers' therapy.

Carl Rogers believed that people had the ability of self-actualization. He saw that everyone had something which allowed them to find their own path without much help from others and gave them the ability to live a good life. Carl Rogers asserted that people experience mental health issues when this ability is blocked off due to some cause, and that if a therapist helps them at that time, this ability would return, and they would be able to resolve their problems themselves. The thing he emphasized most in the treatment process is that if the therapist sufficiently respects, accepts, and empathizes with the emotions a client expresses, whatever it may be, the client will be able to exhibit their own ability. In his treatment process, Carl Rogers never went ahead of his clients. He always followed behind them. While doing so, he would organize the meaning of the words uttered by the clients and repeat them back to them. If you look at the transcriptions of Carl Rogers' cases, his clients say the following, "I feel like I'm with a person who really understands me well."

Carl Rogers was someone who researched the effects of psychotherapy very scientifically. Recording the treatment process and analyzing the interactions between the client and therapist, he studied "what brought about results in the treatment." In the end, after he thoroughly studied several schools of psychotherapy, he discovered what made a psychotherapy effective. The matter of "what kind of school the therapist performs their treatment through" is not really important in terms of the effectiveness of psychotherapy. Rather, the treatment of a therapist was shown to be effective if it satisfied the following three requirements, a claim by Carl Rogers which is almost universally accepted in the realm of psychotherapy. These three requirements are as follows:

The first is unconditional acceptance. It is accepting the client or patient unconditionally. It is wholly accepting the client or patient, just as parent loves their child. This means that the attitude of a therapist who accepts things as they are is extremely therapeutic.

The second is genuineness. In other words, what is on the outside cannot be different from what is on the inside. There are therapists who seem like they are very respectful of the client or patient during treatment, but outside of treatment they say that client or patient is weird. Here what is on the outside is different from what is on the inside. This means that the treatment of a genuine therapist is more effective than the treatment of those kinds of therapists mentioned above.

The third is empathetic response. It is empathizing with the client or patient and conveying that empathy well.

What is important is not a therapist's school of psychotherapy, but rather these three things. For example, even if they are both a part of Freud's school, the effectiveness of treatment can differ greatly depending on the therapist. There is the following passage among the sayings of Yabu, the Song Dynasty Chinese monk who wrote a commentary on the Diamond Sutra:

Even if a righteous person speaks unrighteous dharma, they are all righteous. But even if an unrighteous person speaks righteous dharma, they are all unrighteous (正人說邪法 邪法悉歸正 邪人 說正法 正法悉歸邪).

I interpret this passage as follows:

If a righteous person uses a righteous dharma, the result is a righteous dharma.
(正法 正人 正法)
If an unrighteous person uses a righteous dharma, the result is an unrighteous dharma.
(正法 邪人 邪法)
If a righteous person uses an unrighteous dharma, the result is a righteous dharma.
(邪法 正人 正法)
If an unrighteous person uses an unrighteous dharma, the result is an unrighteous dharma.
(邪法 邪人 邪法)

There are no limbs in the dharma. The difference in result comes from the person using the dharma. Therefore, we must always see what kinds of people there are.

There was an American psychiatrist named Smiley Blanton (1882–1966). He was quite well-known for connecting psychiatry with religion and seeing psychiatry from a religious perspective. During a period of 10 years from 1929 to 1938, he went to see Freud and received psychoanalysis from him four times. After Smiley Blanton passed away, his wife compiled the things he wrote down and published a book, called *Diary of My Analysis with Sigmund Freud*. If you read the book, Freud did not use key concepts such as "repression" or "transference" in his treatment of Blanton. What this means is that theory and reality can sometimes be different. This is something that I also experience when I provide consultation, but in a real-life setting, we sometimes have to adjust to the patient. Of course, if you look at it closely, the reaction a therapist has towards a patient's words differs depending on their point of view. Blanton once said the following directly to Freud, "It seems that much of the help one receives through psychoanalysis is through the character of the psychoanalyst. … Even when looking at my own analysis, I received so much help through my association with you, your encouragement and empathy, and your scientific attitude." Freud remained silent without responding to this.

Buddhism Is a Very Complete Psychotherapy

Freud says the following in *An Autobiographical Study*, "Looking back, then, over the patchwork of my life's labours, I can say that I have made many beginnings and thrown out many suggestions. Something will come of them in the future, though I cannot myself tell whether it will be much or little. I can however, express a hope that I have opened up a pathway for an important advance in our knowledge" [2].

And Jung says the following in *The Collected Works of C. G. Jung Vol. 16*: "After what has been said [by Freud and others] it seems hardly necessary to add that I hold the truth of my own divisionist views to be equally relative, and feel myself so very much the mere exponent of another disposition… It is in applied psychology, if anywhere, that we must be modest today and bear with an apparent plurality of contradictory opinions; for we are still far from having anything like a thorough knowledge of the human psyche, that most challenging field of scientific inquiry. At present we have merely more or less plausible opinions that cannot be squared with one another" [3].

Though these references come from an attitude of humility on the part of Freud and Jung, they also show that the two were not completely convinced of their own views. On the other hand, the Buddha does not speak when he is not sure about what he has discovered. He spreads his teachings to the world only when he becomes convinced after seeing again and again, over and over, and he shows his conviction towards these discoveries. For example, after attaining enlightenment, the Buddha says the following about the Four Noble Truths ("there is suffering, there is the cause of suffering, there is the cessation of suffering, and the path to that cessation") in his first teaching,

> So long, bhikkhus, as my knowledge and vision of these Four Noble Truths as they really are in their three phases and twelve aspects was not thoroughly purified in this way, I did not claim to have awakened to the unsurpassed perfect enlightenment in this world with its devas, Māra, and Brahmā, in this generation with its ascetics and brahmins, its devas and humans. But when my knowledge and vision of these Four Nobles Truths as they really are in their three phases and twelve aspects was thoroughly purified in this way, then I claimed to have awakened to the unsurpassed perfect enlightenment in this world with its ascetics and brahmins, its devas and humans. [4]

If we had to pick out a founder of Buddhist psychotherapy, I would say that it was the Buddha. Based on a complete understanding of humans and the world, the Buddha proposed a personalized method to escape from suffering to each person who sought him out, and those who put his teachings into practice were all liberated from suffering. Seeing this occur again and again in the Nikāyas, I became convinced that Buddhism was an excellent psychotherapy, not to be outdone by any other psychotherapy. The reasons are as follows:

First, Buddhism possesses a clear understanding of people. It is not an understanding based on intellectual reasoning, but an understanding of people as they are based on observation. That it is based on observation is important because it means that we can have the same understanding and experience as the Buddha did through our own observation. Buddhism is a system that clearly understands people's body and mind as well as the world through a scientific method of observation, and it resolves people's mental problems based on that understanding.

There are two types of observation in Buddhism. One is observing the body and mind moment to moment as it is as a whole, and the other is developing the eye of wisdom through the practice of Samatha and seeing ultimate materiality and mentality. Seeing things as a whole means simply seeing things moment to moment as they are: a hand as a hand, an eye as an eye, a foot as a foot, anger as anger, happiness as happiness, movement as movement. Even if we just do this, we can understand a lot about reality, and we can resolve a good amount of mental problems. But it has its limitations. Buddhism talks about no-self and how we must realize this, but if we see things as a whole, it is difficult for us to completely rid ourselves of the view that sees self as a fixed reality. When we see the hand as a hand, we will not think of the fact that the hand is something that changes based on conditions, and it is hard for us to think that the hand is not ours.

However, by opening the eye of wisdom through the practice of Samatha, we can be completely free from self-view. Taking the hand as an example, when we see that the hand is made up of ultimate materiality, and that ultimate reality arises and passes away moment to moment, we are able to know that the hand changes from moment to moment. And since we have no control over these changes, we will understand that the hand is not ours. If we cultivate jhāna and open the eye of wisdom, we come to possess a kind of microscope. Just as a microscope can see cells and atoms that are invisible to the naked eye, we can see ultimate materiality and mentality through the microscope of eye of wisdom. A microscope can only see material substances, but the microscope of the eye of wisdom can also see the mind. In particular, we can look very deeply into our cognitive process, and this is what makes Buddhism a very complete psychology or psychotherapy.

Secondly, based on a complete understanding of humans and the world, Buddhism helps us make decisions that are most beneficial to us. By following the path that Buddhism sets forth, anyone can be free from mental problems. We have mental problems because we do things that are harmful to ourselves. In many cases, people do things that are harmful to themselves without even being aware of it. They even think at times that those harmful things are beneficial to them. Understanding principles that are taught in Buddhism can help us completely avoid doing things that are harmful to ourselves The Buddha lived as a bodhisatta in his previous lives, and those bodhisattas never did things that were harmful to them.

This comes up in Buddhist scriptures called *The Jātakas*. In one example, the bodhisatta was once born into a very wealthy household. But one day, his brother died. The whole family wept in sadness, but the bodhisatta alone did not weep. And so people criticized the bodhisatta. They rebuked him saying that he did not weep because he was happy that he would claim sole possession of the family's fortune. To this the bodhisatta replied, "If weeping would help my brother and myself, I would weep. But since weeping doesn't help at all and is only harmful, I will certainly not weep."

One of the Buddha's disciples is Sāriputta, who known to be the wisest. This Sāriputta is also an embodiment of someone who will not do anything that is harmful to themselves. At that time, Sāriputta was known for never getting angry. One day, someone was determined to make Sāriputta angry and struck Sāriputta from behind on his back as he was walking. But Sāriputta just continued walking without being disturbed at all. I wonder if perhaps Sāriputta had thought, "there must be some reason for this" and just accepted it.

When we look at the Nikāyas, those who received the Buddha's teachings all experienced the same thing that the Buddha experienced, though there is some difference in the level of depth of that experience. We can consider all the Nikāyas to be proof of this. The Buddha thoroughly proves this himself, his disciples prove this, and they also prove this to each other. Among the Nikāyas, if we look at the *Theragāthā* or *Therīgāthā*, there are testimonies of many practitioners having the same experience as the Buddha. The *Theragāthā* is about the enlightenment of bhikkhus (monks) with excellent character who have been ordained a long time, and the *Therīgāthā* is about the enlightenment of bhikkhunīs (nuns) with excellent character who have been ordained a long time. In those texts, there are many people who claim, "I have realized the Three Higher Knowledges in the previous night." The Three Higher Knowledges refer to the supernatural ability to see one's past lives, the divine eye of seeing birth depending on one's karma, and the supernatural ability of the complete extinction of afflictions.

The thing that Buddhism emphasizes the most is the truth. As I have said before, this is because Buddhism is a teaching that is based on observation. Therefore, I believe that there will come a day where all the things said in Buddhism will be confirmed by modern science. Of course, there are things that have already been confirmed by modern brain science. It is likely that rebirth will be the last thing to be proven. It will be a long time before science develops to the point where it can be proven. When we look at it this way, we can say that Buddhism has a lot to offer psychotherapy in terms of understanding people. Buddhism's understanding of humans is more proven than that of any previous school of psychotherapy.

Buddhist Psychotherapy Is Wisdom Therapy

The first step to resolving an individual's problems based on Buddhism's understanding of human beings is determining their current situation. We must understand the patient fully by attentively listening to what they say, asking about their situation, and talking with them. Doing this well help the patient feel that the therapist understands their problems well and is receptive to them. On the other hand, if the patient feels that the therapist is talking nonsense without understanding them properly, the treatment cannot be established.

When enough understanding and trust is established, the next step is to apply a Buddhist approach. There is something that is extremely important when applying a Buddhist approach. If you begin treatment having heard some things here and read some things there, you won't be able to get the result you want. The only things that should be used in treatment are those that the therapist has determined to be effective for treatment through experience and verification. For example, there is no problem in saying it is possible for Buddha-nature to be in all of us. However, it may be problematic to say to a client, "You are a Buddha." If you cannot answer truthfully when a client asks you to explain why they are a Buddha, you cannot expect the treatment to be able to continue.

Even when practicing Buddhist psychotherapy, I do not use any Buddhist terms during treatment. Having set up my foundation on the universal wisdom I obtained through the practice and study of Buddhism and through mindful observation, I proceed with my treatment using normal words that even people who do not know Buddhism can understand. Or when Buddhism as a religion might lead to a repulsive reaction or may be a problem, I use the term "wisdom therapy" instead of Buddhist psychotherapy. The experience and knowledge of the therapist is universal, or in other words is wisdom. And so when the therapist performs treatment on the basis of that, it must be of help to patients regardless of their religious background in order for it to be established. This is why it is called wisdom therapy. Also, since Buddhism is actually wisdom, seeing Buddhist psychotherapy and wisdom therapy as the same is not far off the mark.

The strength of Buddhism in psychotherapy is in seeing human existence itself as suffering and proposing a path of freedom from it. If this is the case, why is human existence suffering? It is because what we want and reality tend to go against each other. We suffer because when we want to be alone, we are surrounded by people, and when we do not want to be alone, we are alone. We suffer because we want recognition but do not get it, and struggle because we gain weight when we do not want to. There are tons of these examples everywhere. It is hard enough to be in stuck in a situation of such endless suffering, but in those situations, we habitually become angry with ourselves and with others. Sparks of suffering fly in all directions, causing everything to be engulfed in the flames of suffering.

Since we suffer from things not going the way we want them to, the Buddhist treatment to this is eliminating the discrepancy between what we want and reality, thereby allowing us to escaping from suffering. Therefore, Buddhism emphasizes seeing reality clearly as it is. It means seeing it clearly and not wishing for things that will not happen. Seeing clearly is seeing and knowing the way the world works, the properties of our body and mind, and the conditions that surround us as they are. But doing this is not easy. Why is this?

Buddhism explains that because we are bound by greed, anger, and ignorance, we are unable to see reality as it is. We therefore wish for things that are unrealizable, and become angry when things do not go according to our wishes. These are called the three poisons (Pāli akusala-mūla), and I consider ignorance to be the foremost among them. What this means is that not knowing how we and the world around us work is the first barrier to seeing reality as it is. Based on that ignorance, we desire things that are impossible. But when things we wanted do not happen, if we recognize that "I must have been wrongly desiring something!" and we observe and realize what we had been wrongly desiring, the links of the three poisons from ignorance to greed to anger will not connect. However, usually what happens at that point is that people get angry. Once they go over anger they are overcome by it, and are unable to see reality. And once again on the basis of that thing which they saw wrongly, they wish for things that are unrealizable. The three poisons are loop back to one another. The Buddha, seeing that normal people live their lives while burning in the fires of greed, anger, and ignorance, said the following:

> Bhikkhus, all is burning. And what bhikkhus, is the all that is burning?
>
> The eye is burning, forms are burning, eye consciousness is burning, eye-contact is burning, and whatever feeling arises with eye-contact as condition—whether pleasant or painful or neither-painful-nor-pleasant—that too is burning.
>
> Burning with what? Burning with the fire of lust, with the fire of hatred, with the fire of delusion; burning with birth, aging, and death; with sorrow, lamentation, pain, displeasure, and despair, I say. (SN 35.28). [5]

The Buddha strived on through countless lives to create a complete system called Buddhism to resolve this problem of human suffering. He discovered the reality of suffering, its cause, and the path to completely escape from it. And so, the Buddha became an expert in "suffering." There was not a single thing that he did not understand about suffering and that he could not resolve. Countless examples of the Buddha treating people's suffering are told in the Nikāyas. The Nikāyas, or in other words the scriptures of Early Buddhism, are historical records that show how the Buddha understood people and by what means he eliminated their suffering. Therefore, I recommend to many people that they read the Nikāyas.

The Three Ways Suffering Arises

Mental problems will not arise in people who live an easy-going life and are happy. If we look at the situations where mental problems tend to arise, we first see that there is suffering. If we examine mental health patients, we see that they have experienced a lot of suffering for a long time before their mental problems arose. These are circumstances of suffering that we encounter while living. Mental problems arise when we are not able to undergo these experiences of suffering properly. In other words, we cope with this suffering poorly because we lack the wisdom to resolve it, or we are stuck in a situation where we cannot get help from others, or we do not accept the help of others even when it is there, and we experience negative thoughts or emotions that are not in accordance with reality. These thoughts and emotions cause physiological changes in the brain and begin the vicious cycle wherein these changes in the brain again bring up negative thoughts and emotions.

If this keeps getting worse, it can sometimes even lead to mental disorders such as schizophrenia or bipolar disorder.

Therefore, Buddhist psychotherapy begins with suffering. In Buddhist psychotherapy, we discuss what suffering is, why suffering arises, and how we can respond to suffering in a way that leads to good mental health.

Suffering begins from the following three fundamental things about humans and the world.

1. The body and mind which we are made up of are not ours. If they were ours, we should be able to do with them as we please, but we cannot control the body and mind. If we wanted to not be sick, we should be able to not be sick, and if we wanted to not be sad, we should be able to not be sad, but we cannot do this. Therefore, suffering inevitably arises.
2. The world moves according to its principles, not according to our wishes. Countless things that surround us do not move according to our wishes. Whether it is other people, animals, the weather, or other things, things move according to their principles regardless of our wishes, and these things affect us. What this means is that when we are unable to adjust to these movements, problems may arise. Since our thoughts about the world differ from the reality of the world, suffering arises when we collide with the world but things do not go the way we want. Therefore, we need to know how we can coexist in harmony with the world.
3. We often create our own suffering. Due to the first and second thing which I mentioned before, we inevitably come in contact with suffering while living our lives. When this happens, if we respond to suffering on the basis of greed, hatred, and delusion, we will create for ourselves a second and third suffering. These second and third sufferings are things that we can control. There is a method of treatment developed in the West that is influenced by Buddhism called Acceptance Commitment Treatment (ACT). This treatment differentiates pain and suffering. If pain is the suffering that we inevitably experience, suffering is not responding to that pain properly and therefore suffering more. The objective of the Acceptance Commitment Treatment is to reduce suffering so that we can do the things we need to do in our lives no matter what arises.

Buddhist psychotherapy thoroughly takes into account these three ways that suffering arises and guides patients to escape from the vicious cycle where we continuously create new suffering by not being able to accept the inevitable suffering, and enter a positive cycle where we reduce suffering. It helps us replace the greed, anger, and ignorance inside of us with wisdom, compassion, and equanimity.

Why We Need to Understand the Cognitive Process

There are two kinds of reality in Buddhism. One is conventional reality, and the other is ultimate reality. To explain using the hand as an example, conventional reality is perceiving that we have "hands." We have agreed to perceive the hand as "hand" in English and as "son" in Korean. But the hand is not fixed in one state. Rather, it continuously changes. In cold weather it turns slightly blue, and when it touches something warm it turns red.

Ultimate reality refers to the things that ultimately constitute the hand. Though ultimate reality is also not permanent since it too arises and passes away depending on conditions, the intrinsic properties of ultimate reality during its existence do not change. Though its intrinsic properties do not change, ultimate reality arises when the conditions for its arising are met and passes away when its conditions for passing away are met. This ultimate reality is invisible to the naked eye. Only when the eye of wisdom opens through the practice of Samatha (concentration) meditation we can finally see ultimate reality.

There are four ultimate realities: materiality, mentality, mental factors, and nibbāna.

When we can see ultimate reality, we are able to completely understand the properties of an object. To continue using the hand as an example, when we perceive the hand through conventional reality, we believe that the hand is ours and that we can do with it as we please. In contrast, if we see ultimate reality, we come to know that the hand does not stay in the same form for even a single moment. Actually, we do not perceive the hand as a hand, but rather see the process in which ultimate reality arises and passes away. And we come to know that we cannot control this process. This means realizing that the hand is "no-self," or not ours.

The same goes for the mind. For example, when we become angry, we are either aware or unaware of this fact. Even if we are aware of it, we only know that the mind is angry; we do not know the mechanisms and processes through which anger arises and functions. If we see anger through conventional reality like this, we will not be able to clearly know what kinds of consequences anger brings to us.

On the other hand, if we see the mind through ultimate reality, we come to know that it is constituted by "consciousness" and "mental factors." These mental factors always accompany consciousness and are in charge of its functions. And we also know that a certain mental phenomenon is not composed in a single mass of things like "anger" or "happiness." Rather, it is composed of consciousness and mental factors and it too functions through the cognitive process. For example, if while turning our attention to observe something we see something with our eyes, the cognitive process that arises is the "eye-door cognitive process." The eye-door cognitive process functions as follows:

Eye-door adverting → eye consciousness → receiving → investigation → determining → *javanas* → registration (may or may not arise) → life-continuum (bhavaṅga) → mind-door adverting → javanas → registration (may or may not arise)

As an example, I will explain the eye-door cognitive process in a situation where the eye sees a flower. The moment the eye sees the flower, cognition begins, and eye-door adverting arises. Afterwards eye consciousness arises, and then receiving, investigation, determining, javanas arise in order. The consciousnesses of eye-door adverting, eye consciousness, receiving, investigation, determining, and *javanas* all arise one by one in succession. One consciousness arises and passes away and then the next consciousness arises and passes away. And then, the consciousness of the five-door (the eye, ear, nose, tongue, body, the five channels of cognition) cognitive process usually connects with the mind-door cognitive process. As a result, whatever comes in through the five doors is perceived and understood by the mind. This process arises instantaneously. Each of these stages are consciousnesses, and those consciousnesses and their associated mental factors undergo the process of arising and passing away.

The part that we must keep an eye on in the cognitive process is *javanas*. This is because eye-door adverting, eye consciousness, receiving, investigating, determining, mind-door adverting are all functioning consciousnesses, but *javanas* differ depending on whether the consciousness is wholesome or unwholesome, explained below. A wholesome consciousness produces a wholesome cognitive process, while an unwholesome consciousness produces an unwholesome cognitive process. In addition, wholesome mental factors accompany a wholesome consciousness, while unwholesome consciousnesses accompany an unwholesome consciousness. Also, while other consciousnesses arise and pass away once, *javanas* arise up to seven times. These *javanas* affect us to the degree that they arise.

Therefore, it is good to know about mental factors in detail. If we know what mental factors accompany a certain consciousness, we will be able to better understand the effects the mind has on us. Table 1.1 organizes the 52 mental factors.

Table 1.1 The 52 mental factors

13 Ethically Variable Mental Factors	7 Universals	Contact, Feeling, Perception, Volition, Concentration, Life Faculty, Attention
	6 Occasionals	Initial Application, Sustained Application, Decision, Energy, Joy, Desire
25 Beautiful Mental Factors	19 Universal Beautiful Mental Factors	Faith, Mindfulness, Shame of Wrongdoing, Fear of Wrongdoing, Non-greed, Non-hatred, Neutrality of Mind, Tranquility of the Mental Body, Tranquility of Consciousness, Lightness of the Mental Body, Lightness of Consciousness, Smoothness of the Mental Body, Smoothness of Consciousness, Wieldiness of the Mental Body, Wieldiness of Consciousness, Proficiency of the Mental Body, Proficiency of Consciousness, Rectitude of the Mental Body, Rectitude of Consciousness
	Abstinences	Right Speech, Right Action, Right Livelihood
	Illimitables	Compassion, Sympathetic Joy
	Non-Delusion	Wisdom Faculty
14 Unwholesome Mental Factors	4 Universal Unwholesome Mental Factors	Delusion, Shamelessness of Wrongdoing, Fearlessness of Wrongdoing, Restlessness
	10 Occasional Unwholesome Mental Factors	Greed, Wrong View, Conceit, Hatred, Envy, Avarice, Remorse, Sloth, Torpor, Doubt

If we say that consciousness is the king, the "7 universals" would be the ministers that accompany consciousness. They are always present regardless of the kind of consciousness that arises. The "6 occasionals" are mental factors that accompany some consciousnesses, but not others. Among them, initial application is first turning towards an object, sustained application is continuously going to the object, decision is determining, "this is what it is," energy is making an effort, and joy and desire are as stated, joy and desire.

In the stage of *javana*, if the consciousness is unwholesome, the mental factors associated with each consciousness among the "14 unwholesome mental factors" arise. Among these, delusion, shamelessness of wrongdoing, fearlessness of wrongdoing, and restlessness occur in all unwholesome consciousnesses. The mind always goes towards some object, and "delusion" is not clearly understanding that object. "Shamelessness of wrongdoing" is thinking without shame even when doing something that should be shameful towards an object. "Fearlessness of wrongdoing" is when you do something embarrassing that is harmful, but you are not fearful of something that is harmful. Shame and fear are control systems that prevent us from doing bad things, but in these cases, they are not functioning. Finally, "restlessness" is where the consciousness has not gone fully and stably towards an object and is therefore restless. The opposite of restlessness is "mindfulness."

While these four mental factors are present in every unwholesome consciousness, if that consciousness is greed, it is accompanied by greed, wrong view, and conceit. If it is hatred, it is accompanied by hatred, envy, avarice, and remorse. If it is ignorance, it is accompanied by doubt. And if an unwholesome consciousness arises prompted by something, it is accompanied by sloth and torpor (haziness). For example, if an unwholesome consciousness arises by just listening to someone else, it is accompanied by the laziness of not trying to verify the truth and a mental haze that cannot distinguish the truth.

In the stage of *javana*, if the consciousness is wholesome, the mental factors associated with each consciousness among the "25 beautiful mental factors" arise. A wholesome mind occurs together with two or three of non-greed, non-hatred, and wisdom, and it is one which sees an object with wise attention. In other words, it is seeing, "this is ultimate materiality (mentality). It is impermanent, suffering, and nonself. It is impure." At that moment, 19 of the 25 beautiful mental factors always arise, and some of the remaining six factors arise depending on the type of wholesome consciousness. In this way, because there is a larger number of mental factors of a wholesome mind than mental factors of an unwholesome mind, we can always make up for our wrongdoings in the past by making our mind wholesome.

The 19 universal mental factors that accompany a wholesome consciousness are as follows: faith in the object that one sees, mindfulness which is aware of the entire present experience, shame of doing something wrong, fear that such wrongdoing is harmful to us, non-greed, non-hatred, and neutrality of the mind or equanimity. Also always present are tranquility of the mental body, tranquility of consciousness, lightness of the mental body, lightness of consciousness, smoothness of the mental body, smoothness of consciousness, wieldiness of the mental body, wieldiness of consciousness, proficiency of the mental body, proficiency of consciousness, rectitude of the mental body, and rectitude of consciousness. When the consciousness is wholesome, the consciousness and mental factors are tranquil, light, smooth, wieldy, and in a state where one can do anything with proficiency. This also means that the consciousness and mental factors stand erect.

The remaining six which occur occasionally with wholesome consciousness are right speech, right action, right livelihood, the mental factors of abstinence, compassion, and sympathetic joy, the illimitable mental factors, and wisdom, the mental factor of non-delusion. When we strive to speak rightly, have the right livelihood, and act rightly, the mental factors of abstinence arise. When we strive to be compassionate and have sympathetic joy with all beings regardless of what they are, the illimitable mental factors arise. And finally, when we see everything as it is and strive to respond in accordance with it, the mental factor of non-delusion arises.

Take another careful look at the list of beautiful mental factors. What would happen if these mental factors were to arise? We would live rightly, our minds would be calm, we would have confidence, and the body and mind would be at ease and would function smoothly. Our facial expressions would be pleasant, and our interpersonal relationships would be amicable. Now look again at the list of unwholesome mental factors. It is filled with things that are hard on the body and mind.

When practicing meditation to observe the cognitive process, practitioners do so by bringing up a wholesome consciousness and then an unwholesome consciousness. After observing how each cognitive process affects the body and mind in this way, we come to clearly understand how much damage an unwholesome consciousness can do to us. After having such an intense experience, we will stop bringing up any more unwholesome consciousnesses in the future.

The Buddha's Analysis of and Solution for Anxiety

Freud talks about anxiety in the 25th lecture of his book, *An Introduction to Psychoanalysis*. While explaining practical anxiety and neurotic anxiety, Freud says that if our libidos are repressed, they will spill out through anxiety. This is because people who are not repressed sexually do not become anxious, and people who suffer from anxiety that were treated with a sexual approach showed signs of their anxiety being relieved. There must be a basis for this since he came to this understanding through an incredible amount of observation and reasoning, and its system is also clear. However, Freud's theory can be difficult to understand.

In contrast, the Buddha's analysis of anxiety and his solution for it is both easy to understand and good to put into practice. Even when looking at it from the perspective of psychotherapy, it has no faults. This comes up in the "Bhayabherava Sutta" (The Discourse on Fear and Dread) of the Majjhima Nikāya. Fear and dread can be seen as being powerful anxieties. When we look at this discourse, we find the brahmin Jāṇussoṇi going to the Buddha and saying, "remote jungle-thicket resting places in the forest are hard to endure, seclusion is hard to practice, and it is hard to enjoy solitude. One would think the jungles must rob a bhikkhu of his mind, if he has no concentration." To this the Buddha responds that he had thought the same way when he was still an unenlightened bodhisatta. He tells the brahmin what he can do to be free from this fear and dread. The method is the following 16 things:

1. Being purified in bodily conduct
2. Being purified in verbal conduct
3. Being purified in mental conduct
4. Being purified in livelihood
5. Being uncovetous and devoid of lust
6. Being devoid of ill will and intentions of hate, and having a mind of loving kindness
7. Casting aside sloth and torpor
8. Overcoming restlessness and an unpeaceful mind, and having a peaceful mind
9. Casting aside doubt
10. Not praising oneself or disparaging others
11. Not being subject to alarm and terror
12. Not desiring gain, honor, or fame
13. Energetically striving in practice
14. Being mindful
15. Concentrating the mind
16. Having wisdom

Through these 16 things, the Buddha was able to dwell peacefully in the forest where fear and terror can easily arise. The opposite of each of these 16 things all arouse projections. Projections are perceiving things that are inside of us as being outside of us. For example, if the mind is anxious, we may think that someone is breaking in and might suffer from severe anxiety at the sound of a branch shaking in the wind. But in reality, that anxiety is not outside of us but rather inside of us. If we put to practice the 16 things that the Buddha discussed, we will become pure internally and these projections will not arise. We will just see and know reality as it is and we will not experience the fear and dread that comes from projecting unpleasant things that are inside us onto reality. I recommend writing down reading, memorizing, and putting into practice these 16 things.

The Four Noble Truths and the Noble Eightfold Path Seen from the Perspective of Buddhist Psychotherapy

The Buddha understood and treated human beings through the framework of the Four Noble Truths and the Noble Eightfold Path. Here, we will look into how the Four Noble Truths and the Noble Eightfold Path can become a framework for Buddhist psychotherapy.

The Buddha himself said that before he discovered the Four Noble Truths, he was in the endless cycle of suffering in saṃsāra. However, after he discovered the

Four Noble Truths, he was able to escape from saṃsāra. The Four Noble Truths consist of the Truth of Suffering (that there is suffering), the Truth of Origin (that suffering has a cause), the Truth of Cessation (that suffering can be eliminated), and the Truth of the Path (that there is a path leading to the cessation of suffering). The forth noble truth is the Noble Eightfold Path. In the "Mahāhatthipadopama Sutta" (The Greater Discourse on the Simile of the Elephant's Footprint) of the Majjhima Nikāya, Sāriputta likens the Four Noble Truths to an elephant's footprint. He says that just as the footprints of all animals fit into an elephant's footprint, all the Buddha's teachings are contained in the Four Noble Truths. This is how much the Four Noble Truths are the most important framework for the Buddha's teachings.

The first of the Four Noble Truths, the Truth of Suffering, states that human existence itself is suffering. Because we exist, there is a body and mind. That body and mind cannot escape from suffering. The second, the Truth of Origin, states that the suffering people experience arises according to the law of cause and effect and that suffering has a clear cause. The Truth of Origin is generally explained in two ways. The first is seeing the origin of suffering as craving, and the other is explaining the arising of suffering according to the 12 links of dependent origination. Of the two, the second explanation is a bit more specific. The 12 links of dependent origination are the Buddhist perspective of seeing the following 12 things arise in order: "delusion, formations, consciousness, mentality-materiality, the six sense bases, contact, feeling, craving, clinging, existence, birth, old-age and death." Explaining the 12 links of dependent origination in detail would be complicated and would make the book endlessly long. Therefore, to reference them briefly in relation to the truth of suffering, the 12 links show us that delusion (ignorance) is the cause upon which we exist, and that very existence is suffering. The third, the Truth of Cessation, states that if we eliminate the cause of suffering, suffering will disappear. This means resolving suffering by eliminating the cause of craving, or by cutting the tail of the 12 links. Finally, the fourth, the Truth of the Path, states that the way to the Truth of the Cessation of Suffering is the Noble Eightfold Path. This means that we can eliminate suffering if we put into practice the following eight things: Right View, Right Thought, Right Speech, Right Action, Right Livelihood, Right Effort, Right Mindfulness, and Right Concentration.

The Noble Eightfold Path is extremely important for psychotherapy. If we look at "The Discourse of The Buddha's Last Days" (Mahāparinibbāna Sutta), there is a scene where the Buddha says that as long as there is the Noble Eightfold path, there is the first kind of ascetic (sāmaṇa), the second kind of ascetic, the third kind of ascetic, and the fourth kind of ascetic. The four kinds of ascetics he speaks of here are referred to as a sotāpanna (stream-enterer), a sakadāgāmī (once-returner), an anāgāmi (non-returner), and an arahant (noble one). These four are what Buddhist call "Noble Ones." This means that if you cultivate the Noble Eightfold Path, you can become a noble one who has escaped from all suffering. On the other hand, if there is no Eightfold Path, there is no first ascetic, second ascetic, third ascetic, or fourth ascetic, meaning that without the Four Noble Truths, we cannot resolve the problems of suffering and saṃsāra. Let us look at the Noble Eightfold Path in some more detail.

Right View is knowing the Four Noble Truths. If you know suffering, its origin, its cessation, and the path leading to its cessation, you will automatically come to possess a mind that is aligned with those four things. You will not seek worldly things, will not become angry, and will not think of harming others. This is Right Thought. If you have Right Thought in this way, you will act accordingly. The last six elements of the Noble Eightfold Path from Right Speech through Right Concentration fall under this.

Right speech is not lying, not speaking divisively, not cursing, and not engaging in idle chatter. Right action is not killing a living being under any circumstances, not touching what is not yours, and refraining from sexual misconduct. Right livelihood is not carrying out a livelihood in a way that harms oneself or others physically or mentally. Trading in weapons cannot be right livelihood.

Right effort refers to the following four things: not allowing evil or harmful things that have not yet arisen to arise, removing evil and harmful things that have already arisen, making beneficial things that have not yet arisen arise, and continuing, increasing, and making abundant beneficial things that have already arisen. It is arousing the will, making an effort, controlling the mind, and striving for these four things.

Right Mindfulness is being aware of the body, feelings, the mind, and mind-objects (dhammas) as they are. This is also called Meditation on the Four Foundations of Mindfulness, and it appears in detail in the "Mahāsatipaṭṭhāna Sutta" (The Great Discourse on the Four Foundations of Mindfulness). I will present a part of that discourse here:

> What are the four? Here, monks, a monk abides contemplating the body as body, ardent, clearly aware and mindful, having put aside hankering and fretting for the world; he abides contemplating feelings as feelings, ardent, clearly aware and mindful, having put aside hankering and fretting for the world; he abides contemplating mind as mind, ardent, clearly aware and mindful, having put aside hankering and fretting for the world; he abides contemplating mind-object as mind-objects, ardent, clearly aware and mindful, having put aside hankering and fretting for the world. [6]

Right Concentration is the four jhānas. Jhāna, which has four stages, refers to the state where the mind is gathered together in a single place. The "Mahāsatipaṭṭhāna Sutta" says the following about Right Concentration:

> Here, a monk, detached from sense-desires, detached from unwholesome mental states, enters and remains in the first jhāna, which is with thinking and pondering, born of detachment, filled with delight and joy. And with the subsiding of thinking and pondering, by gaining inner tranquility and oneness of mind, he enters and remains in the second jhāna, which is without thinking and pondering, born of concentration, filled with delight and joy. And with the fading away of delight, remaining imperturbable, mindful and clearly aware, he experiences in himself the joy of which the Noble Ones say: "Happy is he who dwells with equanimity and mindfulness," he enters the third jhāna. And, having given up pleasure and pain, and with the disappearance of former gladness and sadness, he enters and remains in the fourth jhāna, which is beyond pleasure and pain, and purified by equanimity and mindfulness. This is called Right Concentration. [7]

Now I will try in my own way to organize the Noble Eightfold Path in terms of psychotherapy. Through this, you will be able to understand at a high level why the Noble Eightfold Path is beneficial for mental health.

We said that Right View is knowing the Four Noble Truths. If we look at the Four Noble Truths in terms of Buddhist psychotherapy, they are as follows: The Truth of Suffering is knowing that as long as we have a body and mind, it is difficult to avoid the suffering that arises from the body and mind. Such right view becomes a foundation through which we can accept that suffering obviously arises. This then enables us to not add our own suffering on top of that. When suffering comes, usually out of habit, we elicit a negative reaction. By continuing to add more suffering onto the original suffering, we amplify it. So when the body is in pain, the mind also suffers, and when we have difficulties in our interpersonal relationships, we come to hate those people we are having difficulty with. But there is no reason that the mind must also suffer when the body is in pain, just as there is no reason to hate another person just because we are in conflict with them. This second level of suffering is something we create on our own. When suffering arises, try seeing it as just a part of reality and simply observe it without resisting. If you do so, you will see that the suffering stays for a moment and then passes away.

The Truth of Origin is knowing that suffering has a cause. It is extremely important to know the cause of suffering. This is because once we know the cause of suffering, we can change it to decrease or eliminate suffering. But sometimes, we will not know the cause even if we look for it. In those cases, we should just accept it by saying, "there must be some reason for this suffering." For example, if the body is sick and we do not know why, we say, "there must be a reason why I am sick." This does not mean however that we should criticize ourselves. It simply means that we should accept the fact that we are sick because of some kind of process, and should not be fearful or angry at the fact we are sick. If we do this, the fear or anxiety that arises when we are sick will not arise.

The Truth of Cessation is knowing that suffering will disappear when we do something that makes it disappear. It is knowing that if the body is sick and we take measures to get rid of the illness, we will become healthy. One of the methods I use to reassure my patients is to have a conversation with them based on this Truth of Cessation like this: "There is some reason why or process by which you have become ill like this. If you make a sufficient effort to make the illness go away, the symptoms will definitely disappear." I then propose a specific plan of action.

The Truth of the Path is taking to action the Noble Eightfold Path, making the eight right efforts to remove the cause of suffering. Again, the eight right efforts are Right View, Right Thought, Right Speech, Right Action, Right Livelihood, Right Effort, Right Mindfulness, and Right Concentration. Right View is correctly knowing about one's problems, suffering, or pain. Knowing the Truth of Suffering, the Truth of Origin, the Truth of Cessation, and the Truth of the Path as explained above is Right View. Right Thought is correctly making up one's mind after knowing this. It does not mean making up our mind to drink because we are miserable, make lots of money because we are uncomfortable, eat because we are depressed, or put our minds at ease by harassing others because we are annoyed. Rather, it is making up our minds to exert the right effort on the basis of the Four Noble Truths. It is making up our minds to stop the things that seem to help us but do not actually help us and do things that will help us fundamentally resolve our own problems.

Right speech is refraining from saying things that harm ourselves and others. We tell lies and say certain things because we think that it will benefit us. But in reality, these things hurt others and ourselves, and ultimately cause us to suffer. While explaining the cognitive process, I talked about how *javanas* are important. When we lie, bad things will continue to happen to us in the process of *javanas*, and its results will all come back to us. And if someone finds out that we have been lying, they will lose trust in us and turn away. Right Action is refraining from doing things that harm others and thus preventing harm from coming back to us. It is seeking a path that is good for both ourselves and others. The same goes for Right Livelihood. It is refraining from making a livelihood of doing things that harm others. If we make a livelihood doing things that harm others, it will harm others, but will also ultimately harm ourselves. If we avoid doing this, unfavorable conditions will not arise, and this will be beneficial to our mental health.

Right Effort means making an effort to stop the things we are doing that are harmful to our mental health, making an effort to not do the things that will be harmful to our mental health that have not yet happened but may happen in the future, continuing to do the things that are beneficial to our mental health, and making an effort to do things that are beneficial to our mental health that have not yet happened but may happen in the future.

Right Mindfulness is focusing the mind on the present. There are two benefits to doing this. The first is that the mind will not suffer from being in the past or the future. The mind's nature is to always go to an object. It is then affected by it. Also, it is only able to go to one object at one time. This means that when the mind is in the present, it cannot go to the past or future. Generally, the past and future cause us suffering. But if the mind does not go there, the suffering that the past and future brings with it will not come about. This is a direct benefit that arises when one practices Right Mindfulness. And since the mind forms a path in the direction of the places it habitually goes towards, if we make an effort to keep the mind in the present, a path where we do not suffer will form.

The second benefit has its foundation in the fundamental function of the mind. We can say that the mind possesses "the function of knowing." For example, if I raise a cup and focus on it, I will clearly know the phenomenon that is arising at the present moment. Phenomena that arise in the present moment are phenomena that arise in the body and mind. Knowing this clearly means knowing the properties of the body and mind, and this means understanding that everything changes (anicca), is suffering (dukkha), and does not have its own nature (anattā). When we are able to understand clearly and are able to clearly distinguish the things we know and do not know, we will stop doing things without knowing as we live our lives. We will gain wisdom that is necessary for living life, and we will not fall for things like fraud as often.

There are many benefits to cultivating the jhānas to achieve Right Concentration. Among them, I will present the three main benefits. The first benefit is being able to easily let go of a mind that has gone towards a harmful object. Since jhāna is gathering the mind together in a single place, we must let go of all objects aside from the object of jhāna in order to achieve it. Therefore when practicing jhāna, we will repeatedly train to quickly let go of a mind that has gone astray and bring our attention back to the object of jhāna. As a result, our ability to let go of a certain mind will become strong. Then, if the mind goes towards an object we do not want it to go to or an object that is harmful to us, we will be able to let go of that object easily. We will even be able to easily let go of the compulsive thoughts that are hard to let go of. This means that jhāna has incredible value in terms of psychotherapy. When this happens, thoughts that make us suffer will not be able to plant their feet since we let go of these thoughts as soon as they arise.

The second benefit is being able to stay in a state of happiness while in jhāna since jhāna is a state without defilements. The Buddha even said that jhāna is "the nibbāna of here and now." I see focusing on the present, jhāna, and nibbāna as all being coherent with one another. Since suffering comes because an object which causes suffering takes ahold of us, suffering cannot be present in a state of focusing on the present, jhāna, or nibbāna. If we practice Samatha meditation, the mind will be in a more and more peaceful state even if we do not attain jhāna. It will do so as much as we practice. If you try it yourselves, you can experience this directly.

The third benefit is that when we attain jhāna, the eye of wisdom will open and we will able to see the ultimate materiality and mentality that is invisible to the naked eye. And so, if we know about ourselves clearly, just as I said when explaining the cognitive process, we will not do things that are harmful to us. In other words, we will know that things which are based on greed, hatred, and ignorance are ultimately harmful to us and we will avoid them. For example, if a gambler practices meditation and attains jhāna, they will be able to quit gambling because they will come to know clearly that even if they win money through gambling, it is harmful to them.

As I have explained up to this point, the Four Noble Truths and the Noble Eightfold Path are specific and realizable practical tools that help improve our mental health. Though there are many things in Buddhism aside from these that can help our mental health, they ultimately all fit within the framework of the Four Noble Truths and Noble Eightfold Path. I hope that you will remember them well because they are very important.

How Would the Buddha Have Provided Treatment?

If we look at the scriptures, we find many stories of people who are suffering seek out the Buddha. They talk about their suffering to the Buddha and ask him to show them the way to escape from suffering. The Buddha listens carefully to their stories and proposes a solution based on each individual. As a result, everyone who seeks out the Buddha obtains peace. Since the Buddha possesses "mind-penetrating knowledge" (ceto-pariya-ñāṇa), he can clearly read someone's mind, treat their suffering through a method that is appropriate for their specific circumstance, and lead them to enlightenment. So then how did the Buddha treat these people? I will present three examples of cases that appear in the scriptures.

The Violent Prince

This is an account in scriptures called the *Jātakas*, stories about the Buddha's past lives. In those scriptures is a story of the Buddha in one of his past lives as a bodhisatta saving a violent prince. As the story goes, the prince had a very rough and violent temper, and did not even listen to his father the king, much less his subjects and ministers. If someone tried to stop the prince from doing something evil, he would get even angrier and he would act out more harshly. Because of this, no one in the whole kingdom could stop the prince.

At that time the Buddha, who was still a bodhisatta at that time, was meditating in the Himalayas when he came down to some hill in Varanasi needing something. Upon seeing the bodhisatta, the king marveled at his dignity and sent someone to the bodhisatta to invite him to the palace. He entrusted the bodhisatta with the prince.

One day, the bodhisatta was strolling along the hills with the prince when he saw a small and young Nimb tree. He told the prince, "Take a leaf from that tree and chew it." When the prince took a leaf and chewed on it, he cried out in disgust and spit the leaf out. And then he stripped all the leaves and threw them onto the ground. This is due to the fact that Nimb tree leaves are very poisonous. Seeing the prince like this the bodhisatta said, "Prince, having chewed on the leaf of a Nimb tree, you thought, 'even this small tree has such poison, what would happen when it grows up in the future!' and you stripped all its leaves and threw them down. The way you felt about this tree right now is the same way that other people feel about you. Thinking, 'Even at a young age this prince is so cruel and violent. What would happen when he grows up and becomes king! This king might do something to us.' They will prevent you from ascending to the throne and will drive you out of the kingdom. You mustn't be like this Nimb tree. From now on you should act mercifully and benevolently." After hearing this, it is said that the prince, knowing how to fear the world, became a gentle person.

There are Buddhist scholars who say that the Buddha is the "king of simile." If we look at the scriptures, we often find that when the Buddha speaks, he does so using exceptional similes to move others.

The Woman Who Goes Mad After Losing Her Only Child

Once, a woman named Kisagotami fell into a deep despair after her baby son suddenly became ill and died. She went around the village embracing her son's corpse on her chest like a crazy person, and asked everyone she met if there was a way to save her son. Not wanting to run into her, the people in the village began to avoid her. To this Kisagotami fell into an even greater despair. Then one day, a person who felt sorry for her told her that if she seeks out the Buddha, she may find a way to save her son. Kisagotami immediately sought out the Buddha, told him of her woes, and asked him if there is a way to bring her son back to life. To this the Buddha said,

> If you go down to the village and get a sesame seed from a household that has not lost anyone, I will save your son.

Kisagotami then went down to the village and knocked on the doors of this house and that, asking people if anyone in their household had died. In the end, she was not able to find any household that did not lose someone. Kisagotami returned to the Buddha without anything. However, she did not actually come back with nothing. She came back having come to her senses and having understood the truth that all who are born will one day die. The Buddha then said the following to her,

> Though you had thought that you alone lost a son, the lives of all beings are impermanent. This is the law of death.

The Buddha did not just mindlessly reveal the truth to anyone. Like in the case of Kisagotami, The Buddha would prepare those who were not ready to receive his teachings through a method that they were able to accept. While preparing to learn, these people would realize something on their own, and when the Buddha decided that the time was right, he would tell them the truth. After hearing the Buddha's teachings, Kisagotami ordained as a nun and became an Arahant.

The Wealthy Man Who Is Overcome with Sorrow After Losing His Son

There was once a wealthy follower of the Buddha who, after losing his son and being overcome with grief, did not eat any food for the rest of the week. The Buddha, feeling pity towards him, went to his house and spoke to him. His words are the "Sallatha Sutta" (The Dart) in Book 3 of the Sutta Nipāta. Since it is not very long, I will present the entire discourse here.

Sallatha Sutta (The Dart)

1. Without a sign, unknown is the life of mortals here—it is difficult and short, and conjoined with suffering.
2. For there is no way by which those who have been born will not die. Death occurs also when one has reached old age for such is the nature of living beings.

3. Just as when fruits have ripened, there is always fear of their falling; so for mortals who have taken birth, there is always fear of death.
4. Just as the clay pots produced by a potter all break in the end, such is the life of mortals.
5. Both the young and the old, both the foolish and the wise, all go under the control of death; all have death as their destination.
6. When those overpowered by death are going from here to the next world, the father cannot protect his son, nor can one protect one's relatives.
7. Even as the relatives are looking on and wailing profusely, see how each of the mortals is led away like a cow to be slaughtered.
8. Thus, the world is stricken by death and by old age; therefore, the wise do not sorrow, having understood the way of the world.
9. You who do not know the path by which he has come or gone, not perceiving either end, yet lament without purpose.
10. If while he is lamenting, a bewildered person, injuring himself, could derive some benefit, a wise person too would do the same.
11. It is not by weeping or sorrowing that one attains peace of mind. One's suffering arises still more and one's body is harmed.
12. One becomes thin and pale, and one inflicts injury upon oneself. The departed are not thereby sustained; thus lamentation is useless.
13. Without abandoning sorrow, a person incurs still more suffering. Bemoaning the one who has died, one comes under the control of sorrow.
14. Behold others, too, about to depart, people who fare according to their kamma: living beings just trembling here, having come under the control of death.
15. In whatever way they conceive it, it turns out otherwise. Such is separation: see the way of the world!
16. Even if a person were to live for a 100 years or longer, there is separation from one's group of relatives when one abandons life here.
17. Therefore, having heard it from the arahant, one should stop lamentation. Having seen that he has departed and died, realize, "I cannot [bring the dead back to life.]"
18. Just as, if one's shelter were blazing, one would extinguish the fire with water, so too a sensible person—wise, learned, skilled—would quickly blow away arisen sorrow, as the wind does a tuft of cotton wool.
19. [Blow away] lamentation and muttering, and one's own dejection: seeking happiness for oneself, one should draw out the dart from oneself.
20. With the dart drawn out, unattached, having attained peace of mind, having overcome all sorrow, sorrowless, one is quenched [8].

Instead of consoling the wealthy man with warm words, the Buddha throws a curveball based on the fact that no one can avoid death. It seems that the wealthy man was probably at a level where he could understand what the Buddha told him. After pointing out that crying and being sad is not only useless but is actually harmful, that it is the product of ignorance, the Buddha encouraged him by saying that if he were to obtain peace without attachment by removing grief, greed, anxiety, and the arrow of his defilements, he will obtain sorrowless liberation. What this means is that in order to attain peace, one must let go of attachment and accept the way of the world since one cannot oppose it.

The Three Principles of Buddhist Psychotherapy

I will now present the three principles of Buddhist psychotherapy based on everything I have talked about so far.

The first principle is "understanding the properties of the body and mind." Everything that happens to us is in the body and mind. Even suffering arises in the body and mind. Therefore, when we know the properties of the body and mind well, we will be able to treat and prevent illnesses.

Buddhism says that people are composed of the five aggregates (pañca khandha), namely form (rūpa), feeling (vedanā), perception (saññā), formations (saṅkhārā), and consciousness (viññāṇa). Here, form is the body, and feeling, perception, formations, and consciousness make up the mind. Among the constituent elements of the mind, feeling refers to what we feel. Perception is seeing something and immediately recognizing it. It is knowing things like, "this is a board, this is a mic" and when we see something for the first time, perception puts it into our minds by saying "this is what this is!" This is therefore called the function of cognition. Formations refer to our intentions and our will. Lastly, consciousness is the mind's base function, or in other words, it refers to knowing something.

Knowing the properties of these things, or in other words knowing what they do to the mind and body to make us ill and how we can prevent those illnesses from arising—this is the first principle of Buddhist Psychotherapy.

The second principle is "understanding the way the world works." The world works according to the principles by which it moves. It can move in a different way from what we think. Suffering arises when these principles of the world are in conflict with our thoughts, and if we cannot deal with such suffering effectively, they become mental illnesses. This is because suffering is such that if it arises once, it is easy for it to keep accumulating. And when there is suffering, it is both painful and causes mental illnesses to arise. Therefore, it is extremely important to understand and deal with suffering well. This is the heart of Buddhist psychotherapy.

The third principle concerns what is most important as we live our lives. We must have wisdom to prevent suffering from arising. The wisdom I am speaking of here is simply knowing reality as it is. For example, wisdom about the stock market is knowing the principles by which the stock market operates, wisdom about business is knowing what makes a business successful and what causes it to fail. Wisdom about people is knowing what is in someone's mind, what that person likes or dislikes, what to do to get along well with that person. Wisdom about death is knowing what kinds of phenomena arise at the time of death. Wisdom about birth is knowing about the process of birth.

The way I see it, suffering and mental illnesses arise to the degree in which our thoughts differ from reality. If we see things properly, neither suffering nor mental problems will arise. Therefore, the goal of psychotherapy is to ultimately guide people to see the world and themselves properly so that the things they think of and desire align with the way the world works. This is because there is no chance for mental illnesses to arise if one's thoughts and desires are fulfilled. In this way, the third principle of Buddhist psychotherapy is "cultivating wisdom." It is helping ourselves to live not only in our own thoughts but through wisdom that is in alignment with the world.

In the following lecture, we will take a look at the three principles of Buddhist psychotherapy in more detail.

References

1. Jeon H (2018) Samatha, Jhāna, and Vipassanā: practice at the Pa-Auk Monastery: a meditator's experience. Wisdom Publications, Boston, MA, pp 5–6
2. Freud S (1995) An autobiographical study: inhibitions, symptoms, and anxiety: the question of lay analysis and other works. Hogarth Press, London, p 70
3. Jung CG (1996) The collected works of C. G. Jung, vol 16. Princeton University Press, Princeton, NJ, pp 37–38
4. Bodhi B (trans) (2000). The connected discourses of the Buddha: a translation of the Saṃyutta Nikāya. Wisdom Publications, Boston, MA, pp 1845–1846
5. Bodhi B (trans) (2000). The connected discourses of the Buddha: a translation of the Saṃyutta Nikāya. Wisdom Publications, Boston, MA, p 1143
6. Walshe M (trans) (1987). The long discourses of the Buddha: a translation of the Dīgha Nikāya. Wisdom Publications, Boston, MA, p 335
7. Walshe M (trans) (1987). The long discourses of the Buddha: a translation of the Dīgha Nikāya. Wisdom Publications, Boston, MA, p 349
8. Bodhi B (trans) (2017). The Suttanipāta: an ancient collection of the Buddha's discourses, together with its commentaries. Pali Text Society, London, pp 257–259

Chapter 2
The First Principle of Buddhist Psychotherapy: The Properties of the Body and Mind

Being composed of the body and mind, we are inevitably affected by them. Therefore, if we know the body and mind clearly, we will come to understand why we become ill, how we can escape from illness, and how we can go from an unhealthy mind to a healthy one. Thus, "understanding the properties of the body and mind" is the first principle of Buddhist psychotherapy.

Where Does Suffering Come From?

When a certain problem arises, the most important thing is to clearly determine the cause of that problem. Since there is a reason why a certain problem arises, we need to carefully examine its cause and take appropriate measures. Only then we can change the result of the cause. If there is a cause "A" but we do not deal with it correctly, we will never get the change that we want. Therefore, it is important to develop an eye that can see the cause of a problem. This is seeing reality. The Four Noble Truths in Buddhism are based precisely on this principle.

Suffering can also come from ourselves. The majority of people that I meet in my clinic create their own suffering. The majority of patients live inside prisons they themselves have made. No one put them there. They went in by themselves. Therefore, only they can escape from it. Of course, they may need the help of others in that process.

Suffering can also come from others. But if we look closely at reality, there are tons of cases where suffering comes from others because we did something to incite it. Of course, sometimes suffering comes from the outside having nothing to do with our own intentions. But even if suffering comes from others, there are also many cases where we are not affected by it. Additionally, we may also be able to react to suffering that comes from others in a way that prevents our suffering. Therefore, in the end we can say that suffering is something that comes from within ourselves.

H. Jeon, *Buddhist Psychotherapy*, https://doi.org/10.1007/978-3-030-63098-0_2

One way to see it is that if we can just control our own minds, we can prevent things from giving us a hard time. This is something we need to understand clearly.

It is right to see suffering as something that arises from things that we cannot handle ourselves. If someone says, "I'm having a hard time because I don't have any money," it means that that person cannot handle the state of not having money. If someone says, "I'm having a hard time because I'm ill," that person cannot handle the state of being ill. If our minds become stronger, we can prevent anything from making us suffer. This is a model that we can find in the Buddha. The Buddha did not suffer over anything. It was the same for arahants. Usually, we focus on things like not having money, on being ill, on not having a harmonious family, on society being unstable. However, it can be a good idea to shift that focus to the mind. If we strengthen our minds and develop ourselves, we can prevent anything from making us suffer. Shifting our focus inward and strengthening the mind is what Buddhism is all about.

Knowing the Properties of the Body and Mind Through Observation

Suffering comes from the body and mind. Getting rid of suffering is also accomplished in the body and mind. But suffering in its essence does not come from the body. Suffering arises in the mind.

Therefore, we have to clearly know what the body and mind are. To know them clearly, we have to observe the body and mind closely. Generally, we judge that "this is the body, and this is the mind" through what we think, what we hear, and how we are educated. However, there are many cases where the true form of the body and mind is different from the way we have perceived them. Everything reveals itself as it is in its true form, but at times we either do not see it or are not able see it. It is the same for the body and mind. They reveal their true forms to us as they are. If we can just observe them well, we can know the properties of the body and mind.

It is said that the Buddha always knows and sees. What Buddhism calls wisdom is seeing reality as it is. However, we live not seeing reality as it is but rather in our own thoughts. If we can just see reality, we will come to know that it is very different from our thoughts.

There are two ways to observe the body and mind, namely macroscopic observation and microscopic observation. Macroscopic observation is observing the phenomena that occur in the body en masse. For example, it is observing that we are holding a cup or being conscious of each step of the process of walking slowly. Observing the body and mind en masse can be extremely useful. It can help us come to know the properties of the body and mind. However, it is inevitably limited to those properties of the body and mind at a macroscopic level.

Secondly, microscopic observation is observing after cultivating concentration. The Buddha says many times in the Saṃyutta Nikāya "we can see the dhamma as it really is if we cultivate concentration (samādhi)." There are three kinds of concentration, namely momentary concentration, access concentration, and absorption concentration. If we cultivate concentration, the eye of wisdom will open, and we will be able to see the ultimate realities of mentality and materiality. If we engage in macroscopic and microscopic observation, we can know all the properties of the human body and mind.

What is important here when observing is to do so in a state where we can observe well. It is actually somewhat troublesome to observe things when we are under the influence of defilements like greed, hatred, and ignorance. This is like seeing something while wearing glasses that are covered in dust. We must be able to see with clean glasses. This is the reason why Buddhism emphasizes the practice of meditation. If we practice meditation, we can enter a state where we can observe well even if we are not able to enter absorption.

Properties of the Body

Observing the body is relatively simple because it is visible to us. And so, everyone has at least some understanding of the law of cause and effect as it occurs in the body. For example, everyone at least knows that we can build more muscle by exercising and eating well. On the other hand, the mind is difficult to perceive. The law of cause and effect also applies to the mind such that when we have a thought, it brings about a corresponding result. Yet, this is hard to know since the mind is not visible.

Before looking at the properties of the body and mind, I will touch on one more important thing. Though it might sound obvious, I want to point out that the mind exists on the foundation of the body and is always turned towards an object. Because of this, we are always affected by objects. The relationship of the body, mind, and object is something that we must always keep in mind. This is very important in Early Buddhism.

Now in terms of the body, it has two properties. The first is life-activity. Though it is invisible to us, vigorous life-activity constantly occurs in our bodies. Life-activity is not something that we arouse moment to moment through our own will, but rather arises when the appropriate conditions are met. Once while I was in medical school, I was surprised when I learned about the things that arise in our cells. For example, there is a system in our cells that transports electrolytes the body needs, such as a sodium channel which transports sodium. There are also many other channels which transport electrolytes such as potassium or calcium. All these transportation systems are very elaborate in the way they function. After learning about this, it came to me that there probably is not a factory anywhere in the world that operates in a way that is as elaborate and active as the body.

Such life-activities are neutral. They merely arise according to the laws of cause and effect. While they move actively when we look at their subtle components, in some ways they are like a sack. A sack does not just move to the side. Someone has to pick it up and move it to the side. Likewise, the body does not move by itself either. This is the second property of the body.

Among the two properties of the body, the mind reacts to "life-activity," while it acts on the sack-like body.

Let us first look at how the mind reacts to life-activity. We are affected according to the way the mind reacts towards life-activity. The body itself cannot affect us without the mind reacting to it. For example, if the heart beats with a loud thump, someone might think, "My heart is beating very strongly." On the other hand, someone else might react, "This is strange. Is there something wrong with my heart? Am I going to die from this?" Yet another person might react, "There is probably some reason for this. All I have to do is check it out at the hospital." In this way, we can have a positive, negative, or neutral reaction towards a neutral life-activity.

People are often upset when the body is in pain, and they think that being upset is a given. But is it a given? Actually, it is not. People who get upset when their body is in pain started to react that way towards bodily pain at some point. They did not originally get upset. What this means is that we can change the way we react to when the body is in pain. If we change our reaction, we can accept the bodily pain in a different way.

Some people get irritated even when they get a little hungry. They react like, "I'm hungry but why is there no food? Why didn't someone prepare any food? Ah! I want to eat. But I can't. Ah! I don't like this." But rather than doing that, if they react, "I have a good appetite. Right now, anything I eat will be delicious. If I eat later, it'll be even more delicious," they will feel better. In contrast, if they react, "I am in a hungry state right now. This hunger is occurring in my body right now," they will become calm. We are affected by how the mind reacts. Someone who becomes irritated when hungry will think that getting irritated is a given. They might also see someone who does not become irritated from hunger as strange. However, reacting in an irritated way towards hunger is also something that started at some point.

When there is some kind of reaction towards a bodily phenomenon, it is important to find out when that kind of reaction started. We can then determine how to react appropriately towards it, or in other words, how we can react to it in a way that is beneficial to ourselves. The body may give us physical pain, but it cannot make the mind suffer. The mind is what makes us suffer.

Now, how does the mind act on the properties of a body that is still? The mind moves the sack-like body. This is something that can be understood through the practice of meditation. We can understand this by practicing walking meditation and also by seeing how the mind moves the body after cultivating absorption.

When we observe the phenomena that arise during walking meditation, we find that the foot will never lift itself up without the intention to lift it up. After it is lifted, it will not move any further without the intention to move forward. The intention moves the body. The mind moves the body that is still. When I saw the ultimate reality of materiality during the state of absorption (*jhāna*), I found that the body was moved by materiality made by the mind. For example, when I had the intention to lift my arm, materiality made by the mind came out from the heart-base and went to the arm. When that materiality reached the arm, the wind element from the materiality made by the mind came into contact with the wind element already in the arm to move the arm. Or, when I wanted to speak, materiality made by the mind came out, went to the vocal cords, and the earth element from the materiality made by the mind came into contact with the earth element already in the vocal cords to produce sound. The mind is therefore more important to us than the body. This is the reason why there is a saying that the mind makes up everything.

Properties of the Mind

Now let us look at the properties of the mind. Like the body, the mind also has two kinds of properties.

The first property is that the mind always goes towards an object. There is never a time when the mind has not gone towards an object. The mind always goes towards an object and is affected by it. Therefore, for the mind to be healthy, we must carefully observe what kind of objects our mind goes to and how it is affected by those objects.

But in truth, objects themselves are not wholesome or unwholesome, good or bad. Wholesome or unwholesome, good or bad are determined by what kind of attention the mind has when facing an object. If the attention is wise, that object becomes wholesome and good, and if the attention is ignorant, the object becomes unwholesome and bad. When we meditate, we often focus on the breath, but the breath itself is not a wholesome object. Good things happen as a result of observing the breath because we have wise attention and mindfulness towards it.

To summarize this briefly, it is as follows: if the mind goes towards a good object, good results occur. The mind is at ease, happy, and becomes healthy. On the other hand, if the mind goes towards a bad object, bad results will occur. The mind suffers, is miserable, and becomes unhealthy. The first property of the mind can be summed up like this.

What we have to bear in mind here is the fact that the mind can only be at one object at a time. This has major implications for treatment. What this means is that if we take a mind that has turned towards an unwholesome object and turn it towards a wholesome object, the influence that unwholesome object exerted will cease at that moment and the influence of the good object will begin to exert itself. This means that it is extremely important to try to keep the mind turned towards a good object, or more specifically, to continue to have wholesome and good attention towards an object. No one wants to suffer, be miserable, or to be mentally unhealthy. We try to take care of ourselves, but out of our ignorance and lack of wisdom, our minds turn towards unwholesome objects. If we try to go to Gyeongbokgung Palace but we go in the other direction, it will never appear. Therefore, we must know clearly what are wholesome objects and what are unwholesome objects.

The mind cannot be in two places at once. To digress for a moment, some people claim that they can multitask, such as studying while listening to music. However, this is actually an illusion. When the ear hears a sound, it always goes there. Likewise, when the eye sees something, it always goes there. If the attention goes back and forth from the eye to the ear, one cannot concentrate well. Thus, if we want to really concentrate and do something, we have to just do that one thing.

The second property of the mind is that the mind forms pathways in the direction it continuously goes towards. This is the way that the mind is structured. In the "Dvedhāvitakka Sutta" (Two Kinds of Thought) in the Majjhima Nikāya, the Buddha said that when he was still an unenlightened bodhisatta, he tried to divide his thoughts into two types, namely wholesome thoughts and unwholesome thoughts. The wholesome thoughts were of renunciation (escaping from the worldly), thoughts of non-ill will, and thoughts of not harming others. The unwholesome thoughts were thoughts of sensual desire, thoughts of ill will, and thoughts of harming others. After dividing thoughts in this way, the Buddha said that when he brought up thoughts of sensual desire, thoughts of ill will, and thoughts of harming others, they were not helpful to him. Those thoughts led him away from liberation (nibbāna), obstructed wisdom, led to troubles and suffering for himself and others, and so he abandoned them. At the end of this he added, "Bhikkhus, whatever a bhikkhu frequently thinks and ponders upon, that will become the inclination of his mind" [1]. I wonder if the Buddha felt the urge to continue having unwholesome thoughts after having them a few times.

Later on, the Buddha says that after he stopped having unwholesome thoughts and instead had thoughts of renunciation, thoughts of non-ill will, and thoughts of not harming others, those thoughts led him towards liberation, cultivated wisdom, and did not cause any troubles or suffering for himself and others. The Buddha then reiterates that repetition becomes the inclination of the mind.

One patient who sought me out said that it seemed like when he thought a lot, those thoughts would fill his head and cause him incredible strain. If we think a lot, the room of our thoughts will grow bigger and become full, making those thoughts more intense. I will explain the principle of paths forming in the mind in more detail later on.

Wise Attention and Unwise Attention

Now let us look at wise attention and unwise attention, as well as what a wholesome and unwholesome object is. We need to know this so that we can cultivate wise attention and go towards wholesome objects and stop unwise attention to avoid going towards unwholesome objects.

In short, wise attention is attention devoid of greed, hatred, and ignorance, while unwise attention is attention with greed, hatred, and ignorance. We encounter objects through the six sense organs, namely the eye, ear, nose, tongue, body, and mind. When we come into contact with objects, seeing them as the ultimate realities of mentality and materiality is wise attention, while seeing them as masses is unwise attention. For example, when seeing food, knowing it as "nutrients" it is wise attention, whereas knowing it as "beef" it is unwise attention.

Nutrients—wise attention
Beef—(in a strict sense) unwise attention

Wise attention is seeing objects either as the ultimate realities of mentality and materiality or through the four properties of objects, namely that they "change, are suffering, are not fixed realities, and are impure." On the other hand, seeing objects as "permanent, pleasurable, fixed realities, and pure," is unwise attention. In truth, in order to encounter objects with wise attention, we have to either engage in Buddhist practice or spend time studying Buddhism. If we don't do this, we may think that we are seeing things with wise attention when actually we are not.

Past, Present, Future

To lay it all out, you can say that the present is a wholesome object while the past and future are unwholesome objects.

We call being in the present moment "being present." Being present is not thinking about the present. Thinking "I am doing this right now" is not being present. Being present is turning our entire attention to doing something. Like pointing a flashlight at something, it means turning our minds towards an object. It is a state where the body and mind have gone towards what is arising here and now.

In terms of the past, there are two types, a good past and a bad past. Recalling a good moment in the past is reminiscing about something that is pleasant and makes us feel good, while thinking about a bad moment in the past causes us to feel regret and anger, and leaves us with a feeling that things are unfair or lacking. Among these two, a bad moment in the past is obviously an unwholesome object. Then could that mean that a good moment in the past is a wholesome object? Though it is much better than a bad moment in the past, it still has its limitations.

A person who is faithful to the present, does meaningful work in the present, and is wise does not often reminisce. People who reminisce tend to be those who are struggling with something or need consolation. When one who is absorbed in reminiscence comes back to reality, the present becomes difficult to be in. If we are absorbed in reminiscence, it damages the present. If we repeatedly become absorbed in reminiscence, a path will form that makes it inconvenient to live in the reality of the present moment. I will explain this in more detail later on, but when reminiscing is compared to the benefits of the mind being in the present, the benefits of the former are much smaller. When looking at it this way, I cannot categorize reminiscence as a wholesome object and recommend people to go in that direction.

In terms of the future, there are also two types, a good future and a bad future. Recalling a bad moment in the future is like worrying, being anxious, and needing to take certain measures. A good moment in the future is something that gives us joy and thrill like traveling, a vacation, an expiring installment savings account, or making plans. Then are the good and bad moments of the future wholesome and unwholesome objects, respectively? As we have already seen when looking at the past, they are both in a strict sense are unwholesome objects.

We can only go to the past and the future through our thoughts. When someone says they think a lot, I see whether they go frequently to the past or to the future. If they go frequently to the past, it is easy for them to have a lot of regret and anger, and if they go frequently to the future, it is easy for them to have a lot of anxiety and fear.

Now what about "waiting?" I think of it as being the same as "reminiscing." We wait because the present is not good because the present is not satisfying or fulfilling. It is necessary to change our lives into one where we are not waiting. For example, if you agreed to meet a friend and you get there early, waiting for your friend becomes hard. You may even get angry if your friend is late. You may think, "I got here ahead of time and waited, but what were you doing?' Here, it is good to prepare something to do in case this kind of thing happens. For example, if you read a book, that time will not be time spent waiting for your friend but rather time spent reading a book. Then, you will be much more mentally healthy than when you were hanging your neck over waiting.

Planning is similar. When I was in middle school, I would work hard to plan things out about 3 weeks before a test. I would plan to study the next day and would then have fun with my mind at ease the rest of the day. If I did not study the next day, I would again plan to study the day after and would again have fun that day. After repeating this for a few more days, I would eventually become pressed for time. Perhaps planning is something we do to give ourselves the comfort that we can do something without actually doing it in the moment. However, most people could probably study without making elaborate plans. Of course, this does not mean that all plans are like this. It does not apply to plans that nations or companies make when they set out to do something for example. That is reality of it. The problem here is just thinking about doing something instead of actually doing it.

The power of bringing up a bad moment in the past is very strong. Because we haven't resolved those bad moments in the past, they keep coming up even if they're things we don't want to think about. Therefore, we need to straighten out those instances where someone was unfair to us or the moments we regret. On the other hand, good moments in the past such as reminiscence ends there. Reminiscence arises when we bring it out because we feel like we need it. It tends not to arise on its own. The power of anxious and fearful future is also extremely powerful. This is because these are things that we need to act on.

We tend to think that the past and future are thoughts, and do not consider them to be reality. But if we look at it fundamentally, the thoughts themselves are things that have actually arisen. The past has arisen exactly once. Whether we were slapped by someone or cursed by them, it happened exactly once. Nothing happens twice. It is something that arises once we cannot control. Through our thoughts, we keep bringing up the things that happened in the past. However, we can control the thoughts that arise by making an effort to do so. If we have an unpleasant thought, changes occur in our brain's glucose metabolism and certain parts of our brain are activated, after which chemical changes occur. Those changes then affect us again. When something happened in the past, we were affected psychologically by it and our brains chemistry changed. Likewise, when we think about that past moment, it is also accompanied by those psychological effects and chemical changes though it may not be to the same degree. If we think about that moment in the past ten times, we are affected by it ten times in a way that is similar to when it had actually happened.

The same goes for the future. Though the future is something that has not even happened yet, it becomes a reality during the moment that we think of it. It becomes a reality that affects us psychologically and changes our brain's chemistry. And if we think about it ten times, it will have happened ten times. By bringing up these moments in the future, we are being affected by something that has not even happened. When a physical change occurs in the short term, it usually returns to its original state. However, if it continues tens or hundreds of times, it may result in irreversible changes.

When I methodically examine the process in which a patient became ill, it generally goes like this. They were living a smooth and pleasant life when one day the encountered a difficult situation. They are then unable to overcome that situation with their own strength and are not able to resolve it with the help of others around them either. Then rather than looking into the matter properly and treating it, or in other words looking at reality as it is and responding to it appropriately, they go back and forth between the past and future, stuck in their own thoughts, and are substantially influenced by them. In this way, they are affected in a negative way psychologically, and negative changes also occur in their neurotransmitter metabolism. If this vicious cycle continues, it becomes psychosis or neurosis in extreme cases. It is fair to argue that this principle applies to all mental problems and illnesses.

One of the things I realized when I practiced meditation in 2003 was the fact that "I had tormented myself by thinking a lot up to this point." From then on, I stopped thinking. Then my suffering completely disappeared. Large and small complexes disappeared. Complexes can be seen as masses of negative thoughts that have gathered tightly together as a result of thinking a lot. If we do not think a lot, these kinds of things will not be able to take shape. Therefore, if we are able to think about them less, we can escape from our complexes.

This thought then came to me, "living in the past and the future is mentally unhealthy, while living in the present is mentally healthy." The further away we are from the present, the more mentally unhealthy we become. If we are a little bit away, we become a little unhealthy, and if we are far away, we become very unhealthy. The entirety of the treatment process is therefore getting the patient to come back to the present. I see this when Venerable Thich Nhat Hanh says, "I'm home."

The Principle of Making Paths of the Mind

Why are paths made in the mind? I came to know the principle that paths are made in the mind when I practiced sitting meditation in 2003. I was practicing while sitting down when a thought suddenly appeared. I had not intended for it to arise or done anything related to that thought, but nonetheless it arose. And so I was very surprised. And with my surprise that "I had the wrong idea about thoughts up to now!" I continued to observe where that thought had come from. I came to see that thoughts arise from a huge thought tank. That particular thought arose from the things contained within that tank.

At that moment, I came to know several things. For example, a thought tank is an expert's secret. The reason why Einstein was good at physics was because his thought tank was full of physics. Mozart was able to compose countless famous pieces because his thought tank was full of music. Because the thought tanks of Americans are filled with English, and Koreans with Korean, they are able to speak those languages without hesitation. And so I came to a decision, "I had better not put anything that I don't want to occur to me into my thought tank."

It was then that I also learned that the thought tank has two characteristics. First, the thought tank has an incredibly large capacity. Second, we cannot erase things that have gone into the thought tank. Though we can erase files from the computer, we cannot do the same for the thought tank. The reason why this is extremely important is because something that is contained within us can arise at any moment. For example, let's say that a person who often cheats on their partner practices meditation, meets good friends, does not drink, and no longer cheats on their partner. Does this then mean that this person will not cheat on their partner again for the rest of their life? This isn't necessarily the case. If certain conditions are met, such as the person drinks again or makes friends with other people who cheat on their partners, then they may at any time revert to someone who cheats on their partner. What kind of a person someone is depends on what is in their thought tank and what arises from their thought tank.

I also observed how things are inputted into the thought tank. I found that they are inputted through six channels, namely the eye, ear, nose, tongue, body, and mind's function. Everything that is seen by the eye is inputted. Because our eyes are like high-functioning cameras, they take pictures of things and immediately save them. Things we hear through our ears, smell through our noses, taste though our mouths, feel through our bodies are also immediately saved.

Finally, things are inputted through our mind's function, and this is extremely scary. (The way I see it, the weight of people's eyes and minds' functions is very high.) For example, two people saw a movie, and they were both able to focus on it without falling asleep. In this case, it would seem that the things inputted through the eyes and ears would be similar. But one person may have just seen the movie, while the other person may have thought about it and talked about it a lot with their friends. Obviously, the latter person would have a lot more things inputted about the movie.

If we understand this principle well, we will greatly lessen our habit of thinking that we did something well or poorly. Because in truth we can only do as much as we prepare for. In that moment, we cannot just do something well because we want to.

Things that are inputted frequently inevitably come up easily. If they are inputted frequently, they arise frequently. This is the principle of making paths in the mind. When first practicing breathing meditation, we often lose attention of the inbreath and outbreath. The same goes for chanting meditation or incantation meditation. However, if we do it frequently, we will become good at it. The more we do it, the easier it will become. So when the mind goes to the past or the future, we have to diligently practice bringing it back to the present.

In that case, what kind of benefits are there to being in the present? More than anything else, there is the benefit of escaping from the influence that we receive when going to the past or the future. Therefore, when we can be firm in the present, we can eliminate all suffering. Next, if we come to be in the present, we will gain a clear understanding by observing things that arise in the present. We will clearly know what things are arising in the present. Not only does the mind wander from here to there and is focused on one place, (normally) as greed, hatred, and ignorance disappear, the mind's function of knowing will reach its height and clear understanding will arise. When clear understanding arises, what we know and what we do not know become clear. As a result, we will gain a suitable and clear wisdom that is necessary for our lives. Because if the things we know and do not know are jumbled together, we may delude ourselves to thinking we know things we do not know or do not know the things we know. This makes it easy for us to be led astray. But if these two can be clearly distinguished, we will be able to confidently go in the direction that we know.

There are several other benefits of being in the present aside from these. We will become committed to being present in the things we do, which will lead to many more good things. We will even be able to sleep better. Our expressions will be brighter, and our relationships with other people will improve. We will become confident and gain real strength. Countless good things will occur. Therefore, I consider the present to be a treasure. In contrast, I see the past and the future as honey that is mixed with poison. If we come to know the incredible benefits that the present gives to us, we will not do things like reminisce about the past or dream about the future. We go to the past and the future because we do not yet know the benefits of the present very well. But if we are diligent in our practice to be in the present, we will change more and more and will not go to the past or future again.

The Body and Mind Are Not Ours

We believe that the body and mind are ours and that we can control them at will. However, the body and mind only function according to their principles, or in other words according to the law of cause and effect. Our own wishes and desires do not play any role in that process. Therefore, the body and mind are not ours. They are no-self. No-self does not mean that there is no body and mind, but that there is no such thing as a body and mind that we can control.

We can understand this through observation. In "The Characteristic of Nonself"(S22.59) in the *Saṃyutta Nikāya*, the Buddha gives this teaching to the five bhikkhus who are his first disciples. Let us look at the discourse.

The Discourse on the Characteristic of Nonself (S22.59)

"Bhikkhus, form (the body) is nonself. For if bhikkhus, form were self, this form would not lead to affliction, and it would be possible to have it of form: 'Let my form be thus; let my form not be thus.'

But because form is nonself, form leads to affliction, and it is not possible to have it of form: 'Let my form be thus; let my form not be thus.'

Bhikkhus, feeling is nonself… perception is nonself… volitional formations are nonself… consciousness is nonself. For if bhikkhus, consciousness were self, this consciousness would not lead to affliction, and it would be possible to have it of consciousness: 'Let my consciousness be thus; let my consciousness not be thus.'

But because consciousness is nonself, consciousness leads to affliction, and it is not possible to have it of consciousness: 'Let my consciousness be thus; let my consciousness not be thus.'"

"What do you think, bhikkhus, is form permanent or impermanent?"

"Impermanent, venerable sir."

"Is what is impermanent suffering or happiness."

"Suffering, venerable sir."

"Is what is impermanent, suffering, and subject to change fit to be regarded thus: 'This is mind, this I am, this is my self'?"

"No, venerable sir."

"Is feeling permanent or impermanent?… Is perception permanent or impermanent?… Are volitional formations permanent or impermanent?… Is consciousness permanent or impermanent?"

"Impermanent, venerable sir."

"Is what is impermanent suffering or happiness."

"Suffering, venerable sir."

"Is what is impermanent, suffering, and subject to change fit to be regarded thus: 'This is mind, this I am, this is my self?'"

"No, venerable sir."

"Therefore, bhikkhus, any kind of form whatsoever, whether past, future, or present, internal or external, gross or subtle, inferior or superior, far or near, all form should be seen as it really is with correct wisdom thus: 'This is not mine, this I am not, this is not my self.'"

"Any kind of feeling whatsoever … Any kind of perception whatsoever … Any kind of volitional formations whatsoever … Any kind of consciousness whatsoever, whether past, future, or present, internal or external, gross or subtle, inferior or superior, far or near, all form should be seen as it really is with correct wisdom thus: 'This is not mine, this I am not, this is not my self.'"

"Seeing thus, bhikkhus, the instructed noble disciple experiences revulsion towards form, revulsion towards feeling, revulsion towards perception, revulsion towards volitional formations, revulsion towards consciousness.

> Experiencing revulsion, he becomes dispassionate. Through dispassion [his mind] is liberated. When it is liberated there comes the knowledge: 'It's liberated. He understands: 'Destroyed is birth, the holy life has been lived, what had to be done has been done, there is no more for his state of being.'"
>
> That is what the Blessed One said. Elated, those bhikkhus delighted in the Blessed One's statement. And while this discourse was being spoken, the minds of the bhikkhus of the group of five were liberated from the taints by nonclinging. [2]

We suffer because things are impermanent and nonself. What reason do we have to enjoy things that only cause us suffering? And so, we come to dislike those things, and because we dislike them we lose our greed for them, and because we do not have greed we are liberated. The Buddha's teachings are structured in a very simple way like this. And if the body and mind become fully integrated into this simple teaching, we become arahants.

From the discourse, "The Characteristic of Nonself," we must first understand and realize that the body is not ours. Because it is not ours, we cannot do with it as we please. Through observation we must understand that because the body changes according to the laws of its change, suffering may arise. We will come to know this if we observe the body continuously from the time we open our eyes in the morning until we fall asleep at night. We will be able to see that the body is impermanent. Because it is impermanent, it changes according to conditions. This then leads to things to arise in us that we do not want. Through this, we will come to realize that body is not ours and is not something that we can do with as we please.

Once we come to know that the body is not ours, we will be able to accept things more calmly, even when the body becomes sick. We will not be so down and depressed at our body's suffering. Even when we are hungry, we will be less irritated or not irritated at all. Negative reactions of the mind such as depression or irritation that accompany the body's discomfort are all things that had started to function at some point and became automatic. They are therefore not easily changed. But, if we know that the body is impermanent and nonself and we become calmer towards the changes in the body, we will become calmer towards the reactions of the mind that accompany those changes. This is because we will be less attached to the changes of the body since it is not ours. When we are less attached, we will not interpret the changes of the body as discomfort or suffering but rather accept them as things that naturally occur. Though at first we may have to force ourselves to do this as it may not work well, as we repeat it, we will form a path in the mind.

If we realize the characteristics of the body's impermanence and no-self in this way, we will then arrive at the realization that the mind which reacts to the changes of the body is also impermanent and nonself. Next, we will come to realize that the mind is impermanent and nonself in any situation. For example, let us say that we are in a bad mood after listening to someone say bad things about us. At that moment, we will be able to calmly accept that "If I have this mind right now, I will inevitably have these negative feelings." Once we reach a state where we do not have possession towards the body and mind, we will be able to live a life where we let nature take its course. And as we live reasonably and increase our wisdom, we will resolve the unwholesome things within us and will live a life that brings us closer and closer to the truth.

What we must pay attention to here is the fact that this is a process that we must go through step-by-step. If we suddenly abandon methods that have helped us in the past (despite their limitations) before we are ready we will likely run into problems. We cannot just thoughtlessly abandon things like this, "'When I listen to music, I feel better. But now I won't listen to it. When I eat good food my body and mind become energized, but now I will no longer rely on those things." We have to reach a level where we are fine with eating less for example by engaging in practices such as observing the body and mind while at the same time continuing to make ourselves feel better and give the body and mind energy by listening to music or eating good food. If we jump into water without being able to swim or having a boat to climb on, we will be in trouble, and if we do this, we will make ourselves and others around us miserable.

How to Prevent the Mind from Suffering When the Body Suffers

The way to prevent the mind from suffering when the body suffers is explained in detail in the "Nakulapitā Sutta" of the *Saṃyutta Nikāya (S22.1)*. Let us first look at the discourse:

Nakulapitā (S22.1)

> The Venerable Sāriputta said this:
>
> "How, householder, is one afflicted in body and afflicted in mind?
>
> Here, householder, the uninstructed worldling, who is not a seer of the nobles and is unskilled and undisciplined in their Dhamma, who is not a seer of superior persons and is unskilled and undisciplined in their Dhamma, regards form as self, or self as possessing form, or form as in self, or self as in form. He is obsessed by the notions: 'I am form, form is mine.'
>
> As he lives obsessed by these notions, that form of his changes and alters. With the change and alteration of form, there arise in him sorrow, lamentation, pain, displeasure, and despair."
>
> "He regards feeling as self, or self as possessing feeling, or feeling as in self, or self as in feeling. He is obsessed by the notions: 'I am feeling, feeling is mine.'
>
> As he lives obsessed by these notions, that feeling of his changes and alters. With the change and alteration of feeling, there arise in him sorrow, lamentation, pain, displeasure, and despair."
>
> "He regards perception as self, or self as possessing perception, or perception as in self, or self as in perception. He is obsessed by the notions: 'I am perception, perception is mine.'
>
> As he lives obsessed by these notions, that perception of his changes and alters. With the change and alteration of perception, there arise in him sorrow, lamentation, pain, displeasure, and despair."

"He regards volitional formations as self, or self as possessing volitional formations, or volitional formations as in self, or self as in volitional formations. He is obsessed by the notions: 'I am volitional formations, volitional formations are mine.'

As he lives obsessed by these notions, those volitional formations of his change and alter. With the change and alteration of volitional formations, there arise in him sorrow, lamentation, pain, displeasure, and despair."

"He regards consciousness as self, or self as possessing consciousness, or consciousness as in self, or self as in consciousness. He is obsessed by the notions: 'I am consciousness, consciousness is mine.'

As he lives obsessed by these notions, that consciousness of his changes and alters. With the change and alteration of consciousness, there arise in him sorrow, lamentation, pain, displeasure, and despair.

It is in such a way, householder, that one is afflicted in body and afflicted in mind."

"And how, householder, is one afflicted in the body but not afflicted in the mind?

Here, householder, the instructed noble disciple, who is a seer of the noble ones and is skilled and disciplined in their Dhamma, who is a seer of superior persons and is skilled and disciplined in their Dhamma, does not regard form as self, or self as possessing form, or form as in self, or self as in form. He does not live obsessed by these notions: 'I am form, form is mine.'

As he lives unobsessed by these notions, that form of his changes and alters. With the change and alteration of form, there do not arise in him sorrow, lamentation, pain, displeasure, and despair."

"He does not regard feeling as self, or self as possessing feeling, or feeling as in self, or self as in feeling. He does not live obsessed by these notions: 'I am feeling, feeling is mine.'

As he lives unobsessed by these notions, that feeling of his changes and alters. With the change and alteration of feeling, there do not arise in him sorrow, lamentation, pain, displeasure, and despair."

"He does not regard perception as self, or self as possessing perception, or perception as in self, or self as in perception. He does not live obsessed by these notions: 'I am perception, perception is mine.'

As he lives unobsessed by these notions, that perception of his changes and alters. With the change and alteration of perception, there do not arise in him sorrow, lamentation, pain, displeasure, and despair."

"He does not regard volitional formations as self, or self as possessing volitional formations, or volitional formations as in self, or self as in volitional formations. He does not live obsessed by these notions: 'I am volitional formations, volitional formations are mine.'

As he lives unobsessed by these notions, those volitional formations of his change and alter. With the change and alteration of volitional formations, there do not arise in him sorrow, lamentation, pain, displeasure, and despair."

"He does not regard consciousness as self, or self as possessing consciousness, or consciousness as in self, or self as in consciousness. He does not live obsessed by these notions: 'I am consciousness, consciousness is mine.'

As he lives unobsessed by these notions, that consciousness of his changes and alters. With the change and alteration of consciousness, there do not arise in him sorrow, lamentation, pain, displeasure, and despair."

It is in such a way, householder, that one is afflicted in body but not afflicted in mind."

This is what the Venerable Sāriputta said. Elated, the householder Nakulapitā delighted in the Venerable Sāriputta's statement. [3]

We must make sure the mind does not suffer when the body suffers. Venerable Sāriputta explained this well. This means knowing and always remembering by carefully observing the body that "Ah, these things don't listen to me, change according to the conditions they are in, and cause me suffering that I don't want.

These are not mine." Then, when a change occurs in the body, for example, when the body becomes sick with a cold, we come to accept it saying, "the body is normally like this." When there is a tear somewhere that causes blood to flow, we will come to know it as it is thinking, "when there is a tear, it hurts and there is blood." If we reach a state where we know that the body is normally like this and we do not become agitated at all, the mind will not suffer when the body suffers.

How to Prevent the Mind from Suffering Again When the Mind Suffers

When the mind suffers, we often cause the mind to suffer again. What does it mean for a mind that suffers to suffer again? For example, when a very close friend betrays you, you will probably be very shocked. This is the mind suffering. In most cases, it does not stop there, but rather reaches a stage where hang your head over the betrayal, or you think that you should not trust people again. Some people cannot bear the sadness of losing someone close to them and take their own lives. When the mind suffers like this a second time, this is the mind that suffers suffering again. When the mind suffers, it can suffer again a second, third, fourth time, and onwards in a continuous chain, and when this happens, our minds become seriously ill.

Therefore, when the mind suffers, it is important to prevent it from suffering again. It is possible to prevent the mind from suffering a second time. How is this possible? It follows the same principle as preventing the mind from suffering when the body suffers.

The mind, or consciousness, is made up of four components, namely feeling, perception, volition, and the function of knowing. If we carefully observe these four components just like we observe the body, we will come to know that like the body, the mind changes according to its principles and various factors. The mind is not something that we can intervene with and control, nor is it something that we can do with as we please. The mind that works in this way also causes us suffering that we do not want. Like the body, the mind too is impermanent and nonself and causes us suffering when we are attached to it. We need to know this clearly and apply this knowledge to our lives.

For example, when we get angry or sad, we usually think "I made myself angry," "I made myself sad." However, this is not the case. Anger arises when conditions for anger are met, and sadness arises when conditions for sadness are met. When we develop the ability to see this through observation, we will be able to prevent the mind from suffering a second time. This is because the standard of "I" falls away, and "my mind" becomes simply "the mind." Like the body, the mind is always just there. It just changes according to its principles. However, because we think that the mind is ours, we are unable to accept these changes, which causes us to suffer. When suffering arises along with a mental phenomenon in a person who knows this well, they immediately stop it saying, "the mind is normally like this." They stop the suffering and observe the mind without wavering. Then they see that this again changes based on conditions and will come to accept it as it is. They do not reach the stage of causing themselves to suffer.

When a certain phenomenon arises according to the laws of cause and effect, we have to make a consistent effort to dwell solely on that and not let things go any further. This applies to both the body and the mind.

The Changes that Come from Knowing that the Body and Mind Are Not Ours

As we have seen up to this point, when we clearly know that the body and mind are not ours, we will become more composed with regard to the phenomena that arise in the body and mind. Changing from "My body is in pain. Am I going to die?" to "There must be some reason why the body is in pain," from "I'm so angry I can't stand it" to "There must be some condition for this anger," the negative effects we create for ourselves decrease. Being less angry and less negative in this way are the psychotherapeutic effects that come from knowing that the body and mind are not ours.

These changes also affect our real-life interpersonal relationships. This is because we not only come to see ourselves this way, but others as well. If someone attacks us, we see it as "There must be some condition for that person to attack me." And rather than thinking about taking revenge on someone who attacked or slighted us, we come to analyze their circumstances. We come to always be conscious of the person's present situation, of the fact that if the person cannot change their situation their suffering will continue, and that we too carry the mental structure that can illicit such a response. As a result, we come to see and accept the interpersonal problems that arise among our families, work, and friends as they are. We will become less angry and we will start making an effort to fundamentally improve the situation.

When I observe things in my own life, I found that when the body was in pain, it recovered much more quickly when the mind was not agitated and remained calm rather than when the mind became agitated, anxious, restless, and irritated. When we prevent the mind from suffering a second time, it returns very quickly to its original state. The mind quickly becomes calm and clear. Once we have this experience for the first time, we will make different choices when a similar situation occurs the next time. We naturally come to choose a direction that promotes our mental health.

It is not possible to prevent the body from becoming ill. However, with some effort, we can prevent the suffering that arises in the mind. The bodies of arahants also become ill. However, they do not endure mental suffering.

When the body and mind are in pain, they can be transformed into a moment of enlightenment where we come to clearly know the reality of the body and mind.

Everyday life becomes our practice. This is not very difficult to do. It begins by diligently observing the body and mind from the moment we open our eyes in the morning to the moment we fall asleep at night. Just thinking about is not enough.

Properties of Thought

The mind performs many functions. Thoughts, emotions, perception, will, and consciousness are all functions of the mind. We are under the influence of these mental functions. We must clearly understand their properties. If we do that, it will help us to resolve suffering and mental problems.

The properties of mental functions are all the same. Mental functions all arise according to conditions rather than through our deliberate actions. We just label these mental functions as "thoughts" or "emotions" or "will" because their contents can differ.

The foremost among the mental factors that affect us are thoughts. In fact, many of our mental problems would disappear just from clearly understanding and dealing with thoughts. Therefore, we must become experts of thought. We must be able to help others after we are able to understand and deal with our thoughts well.

We are affected by the things that arise in our minds. When thoughts arise, we are affected by them. As I have already mentioned, having thoughts means going to the past or the future, and if we think about the past, we are affected by the past as if the past event were once again reproduced in front of us. We are affected by the psychological and chemical changes in the brain. Among the patients I have met in my clinic thus far, I have not seen anyone who did not have a lot of thoughts. Most were people who had an unbelievably large amount of thoughts. Even as they faced me, they were lost in thought.

We cannot control thoughts. However, most of us think that we can control our own thoughts. We not only believe that we can decide what kinds of thoughts to have, but that we can choose whether or not we think. Why might this be the case? First, it is because thoughts arise extremely quickly. And so if we do not have an exceptional ability to observe thoughts, we will not be able to see how they arise. Secondly, it is because of the habits in our language. By saying things like "You think about it too," "What are your thoughts?" "We shouldn't live without thinking," "Think before you speak," we almost always introduce an agent that thinks. We are inevitably influenced by such language habits. And finally, third, when we think, usually related thoughts follow one after another in succession. However, we feel as though we ourselves had created the thought that arose in that chain. The truth is that the first thought becomes the preceding condition for bringing up the next thought.

Close your eyes and try coming up with a thought. Try thinking by making the intention to think. What kind of thoughts arise? An attendee: "the thought that I need to go home after the lecture." Before that thought arose, did you make up your mind to have that thought, or did that thought just arise? Were you able to predict that that thought would arise? The attendee: "I wasn't able to predict it. After listening to you saying that we should try and think, that thought just arose."

We are not able to predict what kind of thoughts will arise. Nor are we able to will ourselves to have a certain thought. Thoughts simply arise instantaneously. When thinking of what kinds of plans to make the next day, various thoughts arise one after the other in succession. Are those subsequent thoughts things that we intended to think? The thought of making plans the next day that suddenly arose brought about those thoughts; we did not bring about those thoughts. We are unable to intervene in that process. But out of habit, we delude ourselves into thinking that we ourselves had those thoughts. In reality, those thoughts formed because there were conditions within us that allowed them to arise. These thoughts occur automatically in an instant in the brain that moves at an incredible speed. It is similar to Alpha Go instantly processing the next move when playing the game, Go. If we observe ourselves carefully and consistently, we will come to see this.

The Buddha also said, "The saying, 'Try thinking' comes from convention." This means that we say "try thinking" out of convention, when actually this is not the case. There is a phrase in Pāli, *etad ahosi*, "this was here." "this thought occurred." Even in English there is the phrase, 'It occurred to me.' William James, often called "the father of American Psychology" said that just as we say "It rains," 'It [the wind] blows," we should say "It thinks." This means that we should not say "I think," or "You think." This is because just as rain falls and wind blows based on conditions, thoughts also arise based on conditions.

What are the kinds of things that arise? The things that are inputted in us arise. We can even say that the things that are inputted are "us." Therefore, we must be extremely careful when we input things like a person who has a flesh wound goes around avoiding germs. This is because something may not only come into us, affect us, and become us, but may even destroy us.

For reference, in Buddhism there are four kinds of food that sustain our existence. The first is the food that we consume. The second is contact. We cannot exist if we are unable to come into contact with objects. Things become inputted through contact. Meeting someone or seeing something supplies nutrients for our existence. Third is will. Will is needed for karma, and karma is necessary for existence. Fourth is consciousness. Consciousness is the mind. Without the mind we cannot exist.

Creating a Mind System Without Anger

If we look closely at the outside world as it is, we see that it can never directly affect us. It is our reactions towards the outside world that affect us. People usually think that things which occur externally affect us directly. And so, they believe that if they cannot get rid of those things, they cannot escape suffering. But this is not the case. Even if the outside world remains as it is, if we change our reaction towards it, we can also change the way we are affected by it.

Of course, it is because the outside world exists that we think about it. However, what actually moves us are the thoughts which are inside our own mind. If the thoughts in our mind are positive, we will be affected positively, and if they are negative we will be affected negatively. In fact, having positive thoughts in themselves means we are reacting positively.

Let us suppose that while we are driving, a car that was in the lane next to us suddenly cuts in front of us, making us angry. Usually when this happens, we think that the car that cut in front of us directly triggered our anger. But, if we analyze the situation, we see that there is actually something in between those two things. There is the car that cuts in front of us, our judgment or reaction towards it, and the resulting anger. Then what must change within this framework for the resulting anger to not arise? First, if the car that cuts in is not there, there would be no anger to begin with. Secondly, even if the car cuts in, if we have a judgment or reaction that does not trigger anger, there will be no anger. For example, it is having the following thought, "Looks like the person's in a rush. I've been in that situation before too." This is what we must pay attention to. If we change our judgment or reaction towards an external event to not get angry, then no matter what happens on the outside, we can prevent anger from arising. Buddhism focuses on this aspect. On the other hand, if we do not do this but rather only focus on changing the external conditions, we will never be able to avoid getting angry. This is because there are countless things that can make us angry, and we can only change a fraction of those things. When we begin to observe, we see that the people who keep getting angry are those whose reactions are not mature.

What we can control then is our own internal situation. External situations cannot be controlled. Therefore, when some phenomenon arises, we need to practice assessing that phenomenon quickly and accurately so that we can determine the best thing to do. Since anger arises instantly and we are not yet well trained, it is not easy to avoid anger if we do not set up a system for not getting angry.

During World War II, the Jewish psychiatrist Viktor Frankl was sent off to a concentration camp. In the extreme situation where people who he had shared meals with not long ago were suddenly turned into corpses, he observes a very particular phenomenon. It was that even in a place where people were fending for themselves trying to survive, there were those who shared food, looked after others, and did other altruistic things. Viktor Frankl must have also been among them, as he led a meaningful life in a place where there was not even an ounce of freedom, and ultimately survived. Realizing that even if everything is taken away from you externally, no one can touch the internal freedom of making your own decisions and adopting your own attitude, Frankl created Logotherapy and ended up helping many people. Viktor is said have uttered the following after he learned about the mind through his experience in the concentration camp, "No matter what others can do to me, I am the only one who can do something about my mind."

What Causes Thoughts?

In the "Kaṭuviya Sutta" (Pollution) of the Aṅguttara Nikāya, the Buddha likens bad and unwholesome thoughts to a swarm of flies. He says that just as flies gather towards a place that is dirty and is tainted by a stench, bad and unwholesome thoughts follow greed and ill will. "Longing, bhikkhu, is what is meant by 'pollution.' Ill will is the 'stench.' Bad unwholesome thoughts are the 'flies.' It is inevitable that flies will pursue and attack one who has polluted himself and been tainted by a stench.

> The flies—thoughts based on lust—
> will run in pursuit of one
> unrestrained in the sense faculties,
> unguarded in the eye and ear.
>
> A bhikkhu who is polluted,
> tainted by a stench,
> is far from nibbāna (liberation)
> and reaps only distress. [4]

If we briefly expand on greed and ill will, we can say that thoughts arise when there is greed, hatred, and ignorance. Why is this the case? Though there may be exceptions, most of the time we think because we do not know. People who have wisdom and know well do not think. They do not need to think because they already know. Because we do not know, we have desires, and we get angry, we keep thinking about doing things.

Therefore, if we get rid of greed, hatred, and ignorance in ourselves, unwholesome thoughts will disappear, and all of our thoughts will be cut off in a state of absorption where the mind is focused on a single object. If we look at the Theragāthā and the Therīgātha that contains stories of the lives of enlightened bhikkhus and bhikkhunīs, we find the following being recited by arahants including Sāriputta, "I have arrived at a realm devoid of thought. I am in a noble silence." It seems like the realm of being vividly awake without anything arising as thoughts themselves completely disappear when entering absorption was expressed in this way.

We Can Control Our Desires If We Control Our Thoughts

Being aware of thoughts is not easy. This is because thoughts occur automatically and arise in very subtly and quickly. If our ability to observe is not strong, we cannot catch thoughts when they arise. And if we are unable to catch them in that moment, it is difficult to control the thoughts that arise one by one from that first thought.

Meditation is in general being conscious of the fact that we are thinking. When we first practice meditation, the first thing we realize is, "I have so many thoughts!"

Though we have always had this many thoughts in the past, when we practice meditation, we begin to be aware of the thoughts we were not conscious of before.

Starting to see what arises in oneself is an incredible gain. Whether its observing "Ah, I am thinking" while in thought, or being instantly aware when thoughts start to arise subtly, if we continue to be aware of thoughts like this, we will begin to develop the ability to observe thoughts. The best thing is to be instantly aware when the first thought arises. This is similar to watching a display of fireworks. When fireworks go up into the air, they explode with a bang and then immediately fade away. Afterwards, they disappear without a trace. When we are aware of our thoughts that arise right away, this is the feeling that occurs. It is the feeling of the thought instantly disappearing as it arises.

If we are able to deal with our thoughts well, we will also be able to deal with our desires well. Whether it is thoughts or desire, both are things that arise in the mind, and thus their principles are the same. And so, just as we can catch the chain of thoughts by immediately being aware of the first thought, if we are immediately aware of our first desire, we will be able to deal with the chain of desire as well as the side effects that follow it.

Nowadays, there are people who cannot deal with binge eating or overeating very well. If we observe the desire to eat, we can recognize that it arises subtly at first. If we observe it right then, our desire to eat will disappear and we will not have a hard time not eating. Occasionally, there things like one's sexual urge which can cause societal problems to arise if they are not able to be controlled. This too can be dealt with by observing the mind well and immediately being aware when the sexual urge arises subtly. If we are able to be aware of and let go of whatever subtle thing as it arises, it will not be very difficult to deal with those things.

In order to do this, we must first train to observe the body's movements. Since the body is less subtle than the mind, it is easier to observe. As we sufficiently observe the easily observable body, our ability to be aware will develop and we will be able to start observing the subtler mind as well. Another advantage of observing the body is for comparing it with other phenomena, such as the mind. It can be somewhat more difficult to observe the differences between things of the same category. If we only observe the mind, it may be difficult to see the differences in the mind's subtle movements. But if a thought or desire arises while observing the body, we can see it much more easily due to the differences between the body and mind.

In that case, how often should we be aware of the body? We must observe it from the moment we open our eyes in the morning to the moment we fall asleep at night. If we observe the body like this, how long will it take to discern the subtle movements of the mind? This depends on the person. For some people it can happen quickly, while for others it can take longer.

Meditation Is Dwelling in the Present

In my experience, it seems to be extremely difficult for patients to deal with thoughts. This is because things like anxiety are very powerful. Even if patients are aware of their thoughts and return to the present, they quickly go back to their thoughts. And as they keep going back to their thoughts, they ultimately end up dwelling in their thoughts. And so, many patients will try practicing dealing with thoughts for a while but will think that it is ineffective and give up.

However, it is not ineffective. If we return back to the present moment when we have negative thoughts, we will be affected that much less by those thoughts. Because of this, even for thoughts that seem like they will not ever go away, if we continue to practice returning to the present whenever we have thoughts, at some point they will just fade away. They will fade away as we answer the phone, as we wash our faces, as we walk on the road. And so, I tell my patients to come back to the present moment if a thought arises. If it arises again, come back to the present moment again. Even if you come back thousands of times, you are doing a good job so do not worry too much, do not rush, and do not be anxious that it is not working well and keep going. No matter how much effort the patients exert or how good their concentration is, they are bound to have thoughts that remain subtly. This is because they have so many of these thoughts to begin with. It is important to understand and encourage patients who have such difficulties.

Thoughts arise when the mind is not gathered together in one place. Therefore, in order for thoughts to not arise, the mind needs to be firmly gathered together in a place where it is not thinking. If the mind is always in one place, the chances of thoughts arising are much lower. In other words, because having thoughts means that the mind is going to the past or the future, if we remain firmly in the present, the mind will not be able to go to the past or future and thoughts will not arise either. And so, meditation is an excellent method for dealing with thoughts.

Though many people unfortunately think that meditation means going deep into a cave, meditation is fundamentally the activity of focusing on the present. And if you focus on the present in order to know the nature of the body and mind, this is a truly excellent practice of meditation. We will come to realize things when we continue to focus on the present. Of course, it is not good to try focus extremely hard in an anxious state. Strange things may happen to us. But focusing on the present adequately in a stable state is very good for our mental health.

Because meditation is focusing on the present and knowing the things that arise in the present as they are, the more we focus on the present, the more our thoughts will lessen. Additionally, wisdom of knowing the present as it is will also arise. Our minds have the function of knowing, and if we focus on the body and mind, we will be able to know what the properties of the body and mind are.

All you have to do is to keep thinking like this, "On the other side of meditation is thought. If I practice meditation properly, thoughts will decrease. If thoughts decrease, going to the past and future will decrease and time in the present will increase. If time in the present increases, my mental health will improve." We are as mentally unhealthy as we are removed from the present moment. Being a little removed from the present can be seen as being in neurosis, and being so far removed that you are living in your own world that does not match up with reality can be seen as being in psychosis.

Now we have to choose, whether to think, or to focus on the present, whether to live in the past and future, or to live in the present.

Ways to Control Thought

Usually, we try to have good thoughts and not have negative or difficult thoughts. However, it is actually necessary to let go of all thoughts. I have told my patients that if they are letting go of a good thought that arises, they should write it down if they need to. Normally, it is good to let go of all of one's thoughts. Students are an exception to this however. I tell them that it is fine to think about things that are related to their studies. This is because a student must be able to concentrate on their studies.

People who have good thoughts do not have many problems while they are having those thoughts. This means that while having good thoughts is not as good as being focused on the present, it does not lead to any illnesses. But having good thoughts means that we have established a system of thinking. When something bad happens to someone who has good thoughts, they will immediately begin thinking about it. And so, they are unable to stop thinking when they should, and this sometimes leads to having bad thoughts.

Good thoughts are closely connected to bad thoughts. In some ways, the two are friends. In contrast, the absence of thought is far removed from bad thoughts. If we look at Samatha meditation, we see that the first absorption is close to the "five hindrances" (pañca nivāraṇa) that bring about defilements and weaken wisdom. This is because we enter the first absorption right after eliminating the five hindrances. When we look at what we must accomplish to enter the second absorption, the following becomes clear: "The first absorption is close to the five hindrances. Initial application and sustained application are gross factors of absorption. I will eliminate initial application and sustained application and dwell in the more peaceful second absorption." If we eliminate initial application and sustained application like this and enter the second absorption we will be much further away from the five hindrances.

In order to strengthen our ability to not think, all we have to do is immediately let go of bad thoughts as well as good thoughts when they arise. We should just let our thoughts go, whatever they may be. Our thoughts will then disappear. This is because there will be no foundation for our thoughts to stand on. But since the property of the mind is to always go towards some object, we need a place for it to go after letting go of thoughts. This place is the present moment, something which I have already discussed several times previously.

There are several ways to deal with thoughts. For example, a few years ago I once checked off each time a thought arose and counted how many times thoughts arose at the end of the day in my calendar. In order to use this method, we must at least be able to be aware of our thoughts when they first arise. If we practice concentrating diligently and are able to dwell in the present all day, we will be able to be immediately aware when a thought first arises. Then we will be able to know when thoughts arise.

I use the following method to help patients deal with their own thoughts. I told my patients that when they are aware that they have missed the first thought in the chain of thoughts and have become lost in thought, they should come back to the present and mark it on a card. In other words, while you are focusing on the present moment, the moment you realize that you have missed the first thought and are having subsequent thoughts, you note "Ah, I am lost in thought right now!" and mark it down. I then tell my patients to bring this card with them in the next session.

Many of our thoughts are associated with people. Something that happened with someone or a desire that we have towards someone easily carries over into our thoughts. Therefore, training ourselves to not keep in mind the people who are not in front of us is also helpful in dealing with thoughts. For example, it is not thinking about our boss at work who is not with us while we are on our way back home after work alone.

Going through the entire day without making any noise is also helpful for reducing our thoughts and focusing on the present. Of course, it is not possible to not make any sounds. It means that we should go through the day by trying to make as little noise as possible. In order to do that, we must be extremely focused on what we are doing in the present moment. When we are in that state, there will be no room for other thoughts to arise.

Practicing walking properly is also helpful for reducing our thoughts. There are three factors to walking properly. First, line your feet parallel to each other and straighten out your leg when you raise it. Secondly, tuck your stomach in and open up your chest while walking. Third, make light fists, stretch both arms out, swing them behind you, and move forward with that momentum. If we walk while observing well whether or not these three factors are there, thoughts will not arise much because our entire attention will be turned towards observing the body.

The Buddha said that rather than thinking, it is better to just go to sleep. He said that although sleeping is not very productive, it is still better than thinking. Therefore, if you have many thoughts, it is also good to try sleeping for a bit. This is because it is not possible to think when you are sleeping. However, we must sleep only to the extent that it will not impede our sleep at night. Thoughts bounce around much more at night, and so I recommend that you always try to let go of thoughts when going to sleep at night.

Aside from this, going on walks, exercising, or moving to a different location when thoughts arise can also help reduce thoughts and divert us away from them.

If none of these methods work at the beginning, or when we make an effort but fail, we may have to take medicine. This happens to people who have had so many negative thoughts that they are unable to make a sound effort to deal with thoughts by themselves. One patient who was struggling a lot with thoughts of anxiety said that although he still had thoughts when he took medicine, they felt dull. This means the patient was less affected by the thoughts that were much sharper when not taking medicine. Therefore, after escaping from the influence of negative thoughts to some degree by taking medicine, it is good to consistently add the practice returning to the present moment.

The Nature of Regret

There are two kinds of regret. One is the regret of not doing something we should have done, and the other is the regret of doing something that we should not have done.

If we look at regret closely, we can see that there is greed, hatred, and ignorance inside it. First, the kind of ignorance is one where we are not able to properly see regret arising. And greed is that of wanting to have done something or wanting to have not done something. Finally, hatred is hatred towards not having done something or having done something. Among these three, we will take a closer look at ignorance because is the basis of regret.

If we carefully observe regretful people, we see that they believe that both options were possible at the moment of the incident they regret. They believe that they were able to do the thing that they did not and not do the thing that they did, but that they were too stupid to do so. This is the kind of thought that underlies regret. But if we look closely at that very moment, there is only the thing that we have done. There is no alternative. What this means is that we had no choice but to do the things we did. We went through the process of inevitably doing that thing we did in that moment. But as we are unable to see this, we continuously give ourselves a hard time through our thoughts.

But what would happen if we knew that at that moment, there was not another choice, that we had to do what we did or not do what we did not do? What would happen if we knew that at that time, there was not even the possibility of going down another path? It would be impossible for regret to arise. When we look at it closely, this is actually the case. At that time, there was not another path. Regret arises because of our ignorance of not being able to see this.

For example, let us say that a boxer was knocked out after receiving a counter-punch during a match. The next day, he watches the film of the match, and while looking at the moment he was knocked out, he thinks "Ah, I should have dodged it like this…" and he has regret. But does this work? If it were possible, he would have avoided it back then. What this means is that at that time, this was bound to happen. What he needs to do in order to not be knocked out next time when fighting such a fast opponent is to practice hard. He needs to create a system of being able to dodge the punch at that moment to dodge it next time. In order to not feel regret, we need to continuously practice seeing properly. If we always focus on the present and observe subtle mental phenomena, we will come to know that regret is unbeneficial. If we are able to see properly, we will not feel regret even if we try.

True Reflection

The fact that we are reflecting on ourselves means that something is wrong. Reflecting is doing something wrong and then thinking "I did something wrong. I shouldn't do this again." But if we look at people, in many cases they reflect on themselves and still make the same mistakes. This is a difficult situation. When we reflect on ourselves, we must strive for it to be true reflection.

True reflection is establishing a system where we will not make the same mistakes again. There is much we have to do for this to happen. First, we must see clearly, and then we need to take the appropriate measures. However, from my observation, people usually get exhausted just from reflecting. Everyone, doing it to exhaustion is not doing it the right way. This means we are not being wise.

I will explain this through an example. I arranged a psychotherapy appointment with a certain college student at 9:10 am. But the student did not show up at the agreed upon time. When the nurse called, the student said, "I just woke up from this phone call."

In this case, if the student were to reflect properly, she would first have asked the following question: "Why wasn't I able to get up at this time?" Then, she would have established a system based on the results of her careful reflection, such as setting up the conditions to be able to get up early in the morning. She would be reflecting on her experience and setting up the conditions that work for to get up early, whether that means sleeping earlier the night before or not overeating at night. Therefore, the answer to the question above should move towards figuring out, "I should do this in order to wake up early next time" and putting that into practice.

However, when I met this student and talked to her, she did not think this far. She only focused one the thought, "Ah! You must be so disappointed." and was having a hard time. And so I told her, "I'm not disappointed. I just think we should look together at why you weren't able to get up early and how you can wake up on time next time."

We do not need some big event to change our lives. If there is something wrong with the things that are happening to us right now, we should start by fixing those things. If we keep being late to meetings, we need to do something so that we are not late. If we eat too much food, we need to look at why we do this and address its cause. By fixing the things that we can see clearly one at a time in this way, we can make it so we will not have to reflect on anything. If all we do is keep reflecting however, that might form its own path and become a habit. And so, we need to be able to see exactly what arises with us.

Properties of Will

Among the functions of the mind, the one that influences us the most after thinking is will. Therefore, it is very important to know exactly what will is. If we clearly understand will, we will be able to know well how we should live, or how we can solve our problems.

When talking about will, we often use the phrase "free will." We say that we are "exercising free will" when we think and act based on the will inside of us, without being under the pressure of someone else. If this is what we call "free will," then free will definitely exists. This is undeniable.

But if we are speaking of "free will" as being able to do whatever we want regardless of what conditions there are, or of being able to exert any kind of will, I argue that there is no free will. There is no will that is free from conditions. Buddhism as I understand it speaks of the law of cause and effect. This means that when a certain phenomenon arises, there must be a condition for it. Based on Buddhist scriptures, we can imagine the following conversation about causation. This is an imaginary conversation where the Buddha answers questions that someone asks him.

> "Is there a house?"
> "This is not the case."
> "Is there no house?"
> "This is not the case."
> "Is there no house and is there not no house?"
> "This is not the case."
> "Is there a house and is there not a house?"
> "This is not the case?"
> "Then what is it?"
> "Due to conditions, there is a house, and due to conditions, there is no house."

We are deluding ourselves on a phenomenal level when we say that something is there or is not there without providing any conditions. Even by just observing the body and mind, I was able to know that there is no will that is free from conditions. And while practicing Samatha and Vipassanā meditation in the Pa Auk tradition, I was able to see that when a certain mental phenomenon arises, it is accompanied by its associated conditions. And I saw that if it were missing even one of those conditions, it would not be able to arise. After seeing this clearly, I came to know that there is no literal free will. Because this understanding came from observing, it might be hard to grasp without observing.

If we observe will carefully, we can see that like thoughts, will also arises momentarily. It is not something that we bring up ourselves, but rather it arises based on its conditions. It arises under the influence of our internal state. Everyone, close your eyes now and try to exert will. What happens? Can you exert the will that you want? Please raise your hand if you can.

According to my own observations, will arises in the same way that thoughts do. By practicing to observe the things that arise in the body and mind moment to moment, I was able to see that it was not I who was thinking. Rather, thoughts arose according to their conditions. However, I still wondered whether will is something that I exert. And so, I decided, "let's try going about an entire day exerting will." I then tried to exert this kind of will and that kind of will, but I was not able to do so. Furthermore, if our attention is focused intently on a certain object, will does not arise. In a case such as absorption where the mind has completely gone towards an object of meditation, it is impossible to exert will because the conditions for will to arise are not present.

There are various kinds of mental functions. Thoughts, will, feelings, emotions, perception, and consciousness are all mental functions. The way I see it, the properties of all of these mental functions are the same. Though their properties are the same, they are given different names because their contents are different. When we look at their properties closely, they are all mental phenomena that arise according to their conditions. To understand this properly, we have to observe ourselves diligently. If we practice diligently like this, we will develop the ability to observe and we will be able to clearly see what mental phenomena are.

Usually, we think that we have to want to do something in order to do it. And so, we live our lives saying to ourselves, "I don't want to do this. I'll do this when I want to." But the way I see it, the reason why that desire is not there is because the conditions for it to arise are absent. As long as those conditions do not change, we will continue to not want to do this thing, and our situation may become more and more worse. If we know and see such properties of will, we can see that waiting until we want to do something is an extremely passive attitude. And we will also be unable to predict whether or not that desire will arise. Therefore, rather than thoughtlessly waiting, we should change our conditions by doing the things we need to do. For example, if you do not want to study, rather than having an attitude of waiting until you want to study before starting, it is better to look for various conditions that will help you want to study, such as going to a place where you can study better if you are unable to study at home.

It is extremely important to change our conditions. Let us say that a patient suffering from depression came to me. When we are depressed, we do not want to do anything. Telling that person to do something is an extremely burdensome request. Not only that, but that patient may also blame themselves and think, "I can't even do this!" Therefore, I usually say the following to patients struggling with depression: "Don't do it if it's too hard. But if you don't do it, you should try to do what you can." If we start something this way, new conditions will be formed. Generally, we are good at doing things we have done a lot. Likewise, we can become more used to doing things even if we force ourselves to do them.

The Correct Understanding of Will

When I say that will is not something that we can control, people usually misunderstand. They usually misunderstand this as being "fatalism." They resist thinking that saying that there is no will that is free from conditions means that "human beings can only live based on fixed conditions."

Are human beings only able to live based on fixed conditions? If you understand Buddhism, you would answer no. This is because Buddhism says that conditions constantly change. Buddhism sees that causes and effects are intertwined in such complicated ways that we cannot understand them. Buddhism calls this "kamma (karma)," and if we look at "Inconceivable Matters" in the Aṅguttara Nikāya (AN 4.77), kamma is listed as one of four things that we are unable to understand. This means that if we try to understand kamma, either our heads would explode, or we would go crazy. Buddhism does not speak of fatalism, but rather the law of cause and effect. Our minds, the nature of our minds is such. Fatalism has no place in a Buddhist worldview where nothing is fixed and everything changes and is impermanent. Because we do not know this very well, people ask the following: "Since there is no will (free from conditions), doesn't this mean that I don't have to make an effort to live a good life?" On the contrary, we need to see it as "since there is no free will, we have to make an incredible effort."

For example, let us say that when a monk tells someone to "do wholesome things and practice diligently," that person thinks to himself or herself, "how can I do that when there is no free will?" But if we look carefully at that logic, if we had free will, there would be no need for the monk to say this. All we have to do is exert the will to practice and do wholesome things, and then we would just do those things. But as you all might know from experience, this does not just happen. Such words from a respected monk become a new condition that affects someone, and the seeds of change germinate from there.

We need to understand this well. That is, the fact that there is no free will means that conditions are extremely important, and we have to exert incredible effort in order to create good conditions. When the Pa Auk Sayadaw came to Korea in 2006, I once asked him the following question related to this: "According to my observations, will is also affected by certain conditions. If this is the case, what things that we do become the most beneficial conditions in our lives? What should we do in order to live a good life?" In response, the Pa Auk Sayadaw said, "Meeting the Buddha is the best thing."

When we do something, we can only do it within our own limitations. And so we keep spinning around the hamster wheel. In many cases, the conditions for transcending our own limitations come from the outside. This means that meeting a remarkable person or a person who affects us in a good way can be extremely important. In the "Ānanda Sutta" of the Saṃyutta Nikāya (SN 8.4), it also says "formations (will, intention) come from others, not from oneself." There was once a person named Vangisa who was the best at reciting poems. One day not long after he ordained, he went out for alms when he saw a woman and was overcome with sensual desire. And so he requested Ānanda to help him escape from that desire. Ānanda then said, "See formations as other, as suffering, as nonself. Don't see the desire to do something as being created by you. See it as something that arose based on some condition, and control your mind."

A Scientific Experiment on Free Will

In the book *What is Your Dangerous Idea?*, biologist Eric Kandel discusses the results of scientists' research on free will. According to him, neuroscientist Hermann von Helmholtz argued for the concept of "unconscious inference" back in the 1860s. After measuring the electric signals that are generated in the nervous system, he discovered that among the activities which arise in the brain, a considerable number arise before the conscious perception of objects during the unconscious.

About a 100 years later in 1986, Benjamin Libet put forth results from experiments that supported Helmholtz's claims. He told his test subjects to raise a finger in the air whenever they wanted. He then attached electrodes to the participants' heads and measured the time between when the finger went up and when the electric signal occurred in the brain. It was measured that preparatory signals occurred one second before the finger went up. Then, when he compared the time between when the participant decided to raise a finger to the time when the preparatory signal occurred, he found that the preparatory signal occurred half a second before the participants' decision to raise the finger.

How should we interpret this? I understand this experiment to be supporting the Buddhist explanation on will. Certain conditions arise that cause the finger to be raised, and our consciousness recognizes this afterwards. This means that although we think that we freely exert the will to raise a finger, it is actually the result of already formed conditions.

Let us also refer to the book *Free Will*, written by neuroscientist Sam Harris. He says that in order for the proposition that "humans have free will" to be established, people themselves must be able to know all of the causes that determine their thoughts and actions and must be able to control all of them. But we all know that this is not possible. Harris discusses one experiment which was done in his book. Inside the laboratory, there are several things including water, journals, etc. The test subject's head is connected to an fMRI device. The researcher observes an image of the test subject's brain through the fMRI outside the laboratory. With just that the researcher is able to predict more than 80% of the things that the participant will do next. In other words, the part of the brain associated with the drinking water would activate first before the participant drank water, and the part of the brain associated with reading would activate first before the participant read the journal. If we had free will, we would be able to perceive and control all of these movements in the brain. However, we are not able to do this.

To understand the properties of will, we can also refer to the book *Wij Zijn Ons Brein* (We Are Our Brains) by brain scientist Dick Swaab. In his book, Swaab says, "free will is a pleasant illusion," borrowing the expression from Charles Darwin. Swaab writes "recent fMRI scans have shown that there are areas of the cerebral cortex in which motor actions are prepared for as much as seven to ten seconds before they are consciously perceived" [5]. He continues by discussing the result of one experiment. In that experiment, "people were given the task of quickly touching a spot that lit up on a computer screen. Their visual cortex worked with great speed.

One-tenth of a second after the light appeared, it fired off a message to the motor cortex to initiate the movement to touch the light. If the processing in the visual cortex was interrupted by a magnetic pulse, the action was carried out, but the person wasn't conscious of the screen lighting up. All of these observations support the idea that the notion of acting from free will is indeed illusory" [5].

The psychologist Victor Lamme provides the following explanation for why we think we have free will. As we have seen before, the brain is activated first before we perform an action. When we perform that action, the information of performing the action goes to the cerebral cortex, and it is interpreted as something that "I" have done. This means we think, "I made up my mind to do this action and did it. Therefore, there is free will." But Lamme understands "I" as functioning as an integration of several stimulations, and therefore a by-product of the brain's activity. This means that even "I" does not exist, let alone free will.

How Do We Deal with Will in Psychotherapy?

After I came to understand the properties of will, there was a big change in how I treated my patients. Before I had thought that you could incite change if you had the will and had tried getting my patients to exert will. But now I no longer do this.

As I have mentioned up to this point, will arises based on certain conditions. Therefore, just because you exerted will once does not mean that you will continue to do so. Furthermore, it is not easy to get patients to exert the will to do things that will improve their current situation. And even if I were somehow able to get them to exert will, whether the patient would act according to their will is a completely separate problem. Of course, exerting will is still better than not exerting will.

In order to resolve a problem that a patient is experiencing, we have to help them build a system that will enable them to do so. We have to suggest things that the patient can do to build this system. And throughout this process, we have to also check on how much the system has been built and help the patient go through the things they are struggling with in a concrete manner.

Recently, I have been treating a male patient who is struggling with his libido. In order to resolve the problems with one's libido, we have to deal with it by including various things that are related to it. We cannot just deal with it separately with willpower. If the patient does not have a sexual partner, he may need to masturbate in order to quell his libido. And he needs to engage in masturbation without harming others. However, problems begin to arise if he needs to actually see a woman in order to masturbate. For example, engaging in acts of voyeurism by going to someone else's house at night and masturbating while looking at a woman through an open window leads to getting in trouble with the law. That person could be criminally charged if someone sees and reports him to the police.

If this kind of problem arises in a patient, it is necessary to deal with it thoroughly. In other words, if the reason why they started having this problem is because of stress, we have to also deal with the cause of stress, and if it is a problem with the process of their development, we have to deal with that. We have to include these kinds of things and deal with everything associated with the problem at hand. For the approach to be complete, we have to set up measures for every cause of a problem and deal with them one by one in detail. And of course, a change in that person's system must actually occur during that time.

In some ways, we humans are like Alpha Go. Of course, we are actually much more complex than Alpha Go, but in terms of the fact that both Alpha Go and humans are affected by conditions and that we both follow the law of cause and effect, we are fundamentally the same. From this point of view, the therapist is someone who proposes ways to change the conditions, thereby helping to change the system. But there is nothing the therapist can do if the patient does not go along the path that they propose. No matter how excellent Buddhist psychotherapy may be as a method of treatment, change occurs only as much as the patient takes action.

The Buddha himself said that it is difficult to teach beings who do not have a karmic connection. And so, he gave the appropriate teachings at the appropriate time. In Buddhist scriptures, there was an infamous murderer named Angulimala who cuts off the fingers of the people he killed and sewed them into a necklace. His goal was to make a necklace of the fingers of a 1000 people. After killing 999 people, Angulimala was going to kill his own mother as the final person. Right then, the Buddha stepped in front of him and reformed him. Buddha knew that if he did something at that moment it would have an effect. He saw that will is a phenomenon that arises according to conditions.

When talking with a patient at the clinic, something may arise in the patient that can lead to a positive change due to the conditions that are set up at that moment. For example, the patient may recall his family's suffering that he was previously unable to recognize. A therapist must be able to use these kinds of things effectively. In addition, a therapist must also figure out what arises in their patient's mind when they go about their normal lives outside of the clinic. This is because we are affected by the things that arise in our minds. In addition, the therapist must be able to determine the specific condition that the patient is in. And when a positive will arises in the patient, the therapist must also be able to know fully whether or not the conditions are there for the patient to apply it. Based on these things, the therapist must be able to suggest an appropriate path at the appropriate time so that change can occur.

Creating a System of Quitting Alcoholism

Thinking that you can do something and actually doing it are two different things. The important thing is to not stop at thinking about doing something and making it so that you can actually do it. For example, in order to escape from alcoholism, we have to make it so that we do not drink even when we see alcohol. Even if you make a resolution a 100 times to quit by saying that alcohol is bad for us, if we then lose control when we are in front of alcohol, we will never be able to escape from it.

The way I see it, addictions arise because we frequently engage in them. In the process of repeatedly engaging in those activities, circuits, and paths are formed in the brain and through those conditions we become addicted. In order to escape from these addictions, we have to not engage in them. Therefore, we have to examine how we can make it so we do not engage in our addictions.

Admitting an alcoholic into a hospital is an attempt to create new circuits while cutting off their links with alcohol by preventing them from drinking by force. However, doing this has the disadvantage of impeding the patient's life since they cannot work if they are admitted to a hospital. In the past, there was a medicine that was used to treat alcoholism called "alcohol stop." Nowadays, it is no longer in production. If you took that medicine, it would cause your body would suffer when consuming alcohol because the alcohol would not be able to be broken down. It would be extremely hard on the body causing you to feel nauseous, your face to turn red, your breath to become uneasy, and your heart to feel constricted. In other words, someone who could drink very easily would turn into someone who struggles a lot to drink. If you prescribe medicine to an alcoholic, they will first try to drink even after taking the medicine thinking that it will be ok. However, drinking would become extremely miserable. They would then stop drinking after experiencing this pain.

How then can you get someone who enjoys drinking so much to take this medicine? Actually, there are times when alcoholics do not want to drink. Generally, they say that they feel this way when they wake up in the morning as they sober up during their sleep and come back to their senses. They come to realize, "How can I keep living this way?" "I've been bad to my family." While the alcoholic is in this state, we can create a therapeutic alliance with them. We can recommend to an alcoholic who has come to the clinic due to alcoholism that they take this medicine in the morning since it can help them escape from alcoholism from then on. Here the therapist forms an alliance with the healthy side of the patient to target the unhealthy side of the patient. By doing this, they are able to more easily cure the alcohol addiction. However, this method will not work for patients whose healthy sides have also been damaged because they will not even want to take the medicine. For these people, there may be no choice but to admit them into a hospital.

To put it in more grave terms, alcoholism is a state where alcohol has taken ahold of someone. This means that the patient has become a pawn to the king of alcohol. If it tells them "hey, drink," they will have no choice but to drink. Since alcohol is like a powerful giant here and the patient is small and weak, they cannot solve their problem by fighting it. They will lose every time.

And so, I tell my patients who suffer from alcoholism to always run away when they see alcohol. I tell them that if they see a bar while walking on the street to immediately turn around and go the other way. I also tell them to have someone in their family remove alcohol in their home rather than having them remove it themselves. As I have said earlier, all addictions are the result of doing something frequently, and so if you do not do those things, the power of the addiction becomes weaker and weaker. If an alcoholic continues to run away when they see alcohol, they will eventually reach a state where they are protected from it.

And I also tell these patients to install a camera at their home and have them watch what they do when they are drunk. Since an alcoholic does not know what kind of person they become when they are drunk, getting them to know this themselves by confirming it directly like this can also be effective. This is because a person must clearly recognize that engaging in the addiction is extremely harmful for them in order to stop it.

When we look at alcoholics, generally we find that there are a lot of people who do not have other hobbies aside from drinking. Drinking is the only way for them to have fun in their lives. There are also a lot of cases where people are not able to express their opinions without drinking. When these people drink, the first thing they tend to do is vent out negative stories. And so, it is also necessary to suggest something better to do than drinking. This means carefully observing what interests the person and suggesting things that are appropriate to them. For those who cannot express their opinions well, it can also be helpful to teach them techniques for expressing their opinions without drinking. So, rather than just dealing with the alcohol, we need to thoroughly understand the patient's life in its entirety and approach the problem of alcoholism from multiple specific angles.

To sum up the ways to escape from alcoholism, we must first run away from actual alcohol, and then completely run away from memories, thoughts, and feelings associated with alcohol. Finally, we need to engage in new hobbies and find ways to fundamentally change our lives for the better.

References

1. Bodhi B (trans) (1995). The middle length discourses of the Buddha: a translation of the Majjhima Nikāya. Simon and Schuster, New York, p 208
2. Bodhi B (trans) (2000). The connected discourses of the Buddha: a translation of the Saṃyutta Nikāya. Wisdom Publications, Boston, MA, pp 901–903
3. Bodhi B (trans) (2000). The connected discourses of the Buddha: a translation of the Saṃyutta Nikāya. Wisdom Publications, Boston, MA, pp 854–856
4. Bodhi B (trans) (2012). The numerical discourses of the Buddha: a translation of the Aṅguttara Nikāya. Wisdom Publications, Boston, MA, p 359
5. Swaab DF. (2010). We are our brains: a neurobiography of the brain, from the womb to Alzheimer's. Random House Publishing Group, London, p 555

Chapter 3
The Second Principle of Buddhist Psychotherapy: The Principles of the Way the World Works

As long as the body and mind function, we are unable to avoid the suffering that comes from them. Yet, we are able to eliminate the suffering that we ourselves create. This is an extremely important point of view in Buddhist psychotherapy. The second principle of Buddhist psychotherapy focuses on eliminating suffering by doing things that align with the principles of the way the world works. If we clearly understand the properties of the way the world works, we will not resent the things we come across while living our lives. What this means is that we will live a flexible and active life riding along the waves of the world.

The Reason Why Life Is Bound to Be Suffering

There are many reasons why being alive is inherently difficult. First, it is because we are just one being among countless other things. There are countless living beings aside from ourselves, and there are also countless natural phenomena. However, these other beings and natural phenomena do not exist for our sake. Each of these beings all do what is best for themselves. If we end up becoming an object of theirs, things may inevitably become difficult for us. Take for example mosquitoes. They have no choice but to bite us in order to survive. However, when they bite us, we become itchy. In addition, we are intrinsically bound to experience suffering because we are inevitably affected by the many things in nature. Furthermore, just as we have seen in the first principle of Buddhist psychotherapy, we suffer because the body and mind are fundamentally uncontrollable. Therefore, we are unable to stop suffering from arising.

In order to lessen our suffering, we have to look carefully at the world we live in. This means seeing what the world is composed of and how it works so that we can live in accordance with the world. If we live without following the flow of the world, suffering will certainly follow. We suffer because we collide with the world. For example, if some businessperson keeps trying to go in one direction while everyone else is going in the other direction, no one will engage with that businessperson.

H. Jeon, *Buddhist Psychotherapy*, https://doi.org/10.1007/978-3-030-63098-0_3

How miserable must they be since the more they do this, the more they will walk the path of failure? The same goes for interpersonal relationships. All we have to do is live according to the principles of interpersonal relationships. However, as long as we do not, we will continue to be in conflict and suffer.

Thus, we must clearly understand things in the world and live according to them. If we do not do this, hardships will continue to build up and make us suffer more and more. And if this continues, mental problems will arise.

The Composition of the World

There are many things that exist in the world, and they are largely divided into two groups based on their properties, namely non-living things and living beings.

Non-living things function in an orderly manner based their conditions following the laws of nature or the laws of physics. Of course, non-living things can also create new conditions. For example, a volcano can affect things when it erupts. In contrast, living beings go about their activities and react to stimuli. If I were to throw a ball towards one of you, the person who the ball was thrown to would either avoid it or catch it. Others would look to see where the ball went. When a person dies, he or she becomes a non-living being. If you were to kick a person while they were alive, they would react by either avoiding it or blocking it. But if you were to kick a dead person, much like the ball, they would only move according to the laws of physics. In addition, living beings consider themselves to be the most valuable. This is an important property of living beings. It is how living beings can differentiate between self and others.

To paint a simple picture of the world, it is one where we, the most valuable being, are surrounded by non-living things and other beings (who have life but are not ourselves). "We" are the most valuable things in the world to ourselves. If I put myself giving this lecture at the center, all of you are beings who orbit around me like satellites along with other non-living things. And since all living beings in the world can also put themselves at the center, the world has countless centers.

Because we have the habit of seeing ourselves at the center, we think "I am the most valuable." When we are at the center, of course we become the most valuable. However, if that center moves to another living being, then that being becomes the most important. This principle does not change whether it is a person or an ant or a mosquito. This is something that we must acknowledge. We must remember this principle when encountering other living beings, and we must think and act according to it. You are a remarkable person even if you can just do this.

In this way, we have looked at the composition of the world. Now we are ready to take a look at what kinds of things happen between living and non-living beings, and through what principles those things arise.

The Interaction Between Us and Non-living Things

First, let us look at what happens between us and non-living things. We already know through experience that non-living things affect us, and that we do things in reaction to them. There are countless kinds of such interactions, and among them the most basic is breathing. This is because although we can survive a few days without drinking water, we will quickly lose our lives if we do not breathe. We breathe in air and after it provides us with life, we send it back out. Sending it out like this affects the composition of the air and creates change, and that change then affects other living beings.

In this case, how do the interactions between us and non-living things occur? They occur according to the laws of nature or the laws of physics. For example, when we entered this classroom, we would have been affected by the temperature of the classroom. The temperature cannot affect each of us differently, such as a 30 °C room affecting me at 29 °C and everyone else at 30 °C. It affects everyone the same way according to the laws of nature. Living beings like ourselves are affected in this way and end up making a choice. We can stay put, turn on the air conditioner, open the window, or we can take off our outer clothes. Whatever we choose, the same choice yields the same result. If someone turns on the air conditioner and sets the temperature to 25 °C, the temperature will drop to 25 °C regardless of who turned the air conditioner on. In this way, the results that come from the interaction between living beings and non-living things occur according to the laws of nature. This means that if two living beings make the same choice, then the same result will occur.

The Interaction Between Ourselves and Others

Now let us look at the principles through which interactions between living beings occur. For convenience, I will explain it as the interaction between one person and another, but whether it is between one and many people, or between many people and many other people, the principles of interactions that occur between living beings remains the same.

Now, let us say that we do something towards someone else. Why would we do this? We do this to survive and avoid suffering. This is our point of departure. For example, if a baby is hungry, it will cry. Whether its mother is asleep or in the bathroom, whether it is night or early in the morning, the baby will cry without any exceptions. The baby informs someone of its hunger because it is unable to take care of its own food. What would happen if the baby did not cry? It would be hungry and suffer. And what would happen if it continued to not cry? Of course, the mother would probably feed it when the time comes, but let us suppose here that this does not happen. The baby would end up dying of starvation.

If a living being stays put, it will suffer and eventually die. This is because living beings have no choice but to do something to keep themselves alive from the moment they are born until they die. We can say that this is also the suffering that Buddhism refers to. We cannot be self-sufficient. In other words, we need others. Though nowadays it may not seem like we need the help of others to survive since we can get the things we want right away by just clicking a few times on the internet, fundamentally we are beings that have no choice but to live together with others.

Take a look at the actions you take towards others. If you do this, you will realize that all the actions you take are for your own sake. This is an unchanging point of departure. It is just that our actions can look good or bad to others. Some of you might have the following question in regard to what I am saying: "Isn't a parent who jumps into the water to save a drowning child not acting for their own sake but for the sake of the child?" This is not the case. Parents act this way because it is better for them to risk their lives and jump into the water than to see the child drown in the water.

When counseling patients, some patients say things like "so-and-so is taking care of themselves" and see that they are in a negative light. However, taking care of oneself is not wrong. It is alright for everyone to take care of themselves. Someone who is hurt by this and criticizes those actions lacks understanding. However, while taking care of ourselves, there are a few things that we must try to uphold, such as not taking care of ourselves at the expense of others. When someone does something for themselves, we can speak to whether they do so with wisdom or with ignorance.

Our actions are the cause and will bring about their respective effects. Whether our actions become a good cause or a bad cause depends entirely upon the judgment of others. This means that the characteristic of the result is determined by the judgment of others. Actions that benefit ourselves and others lead to favorable results. On the other hand, actions that benefit ourselves but not others are met with resistance. Such is the law among living beings. In conclusion, we can say that things which benefit both self and others are good, while things which benefit self but not others are bad.

Among good and bad things, they range from small to large. And this of course is also determined by the judgments of others. For example, let us say that we went to someone's wedding. While we would not just go to anyone's wedding, if we presume that some wedding hosts would welcome us while others would avoid us, going to a wedding of someone who welcomes us is good, while going to a wedding of someone who avoids us is bad. And of course, the degree of good or bad would be determined by how much the host's emotions are affected. In this overall context, what then is the worst thing that we can do? It is killing. Living beings do not want to die, and therefore killing is the greatest evil. It is also the reason why murder is dealt with most severely by the law. On the other hand, the greatest good that one can do in the same vein is saving the life of a dying person.

Good actions lead to favorable results and bring us joy. On the other hand, bad actions lead to resistance and cause suffering. Such is the Buddhist point of view on cause and effect, which says "good causes bring happy results, bad causes bring unhappy results (善因樂果 惡因苦果)." Since living beings form societies, the Buddhist point of view on cause and effect naturally expands to the ethical laws of society. It is not a law of ethics that we must follow, but rather becomes a natural law of ethics that inevitably plays itself out.

The Image of Ourselves Within Others Will Shape Our Lives

I will try explaining "good causes bring happy results, bad causes bring unhappy results" in a more concrete way. Everyone here right now probably has a lot of acquaintances. Each of you probably knows tens of thousands of people. There are people you remember, and people you might have forgotten because you have not seen them for a while but can recall if you dig in your memory. Even if we just consider the people you went to school with, there are probably several thousand. All we have to do is recognize that we are present in the minds of all of the people we have come into contact with. Just as whether it is a river or a stream, the moon's shadow can be seen in the water when it rises in the night sky, we are inside the minds of all the people who have seen us. Which version of us is in their minds? It is the version they have judged that is in their minds.

If a good version of us is in those people's minds, good things will come to us, while if a bad version of us is in their minds, bad things will come to us. For example, let us say that I came out on TV. Would a lot of people then come to my clinic, or would few people come? Either can happen. If the version of me as "'someone who is good at psychotherapy" inputted into the minds of those watching me on TV, then eventually a lot of patients will come even if it does not happen right away. Those people will come themselves if they have problems, they will also recommend me to others around them who have problems. On the other hand, they think, "this person isn't very good. He is stuck in Buddhism and can't separate his own interests," there will be no reason for patients to come to me.

I have a dog at home, and so I am also in the mind of my dog. The version of me that is in the dog's mind is the one it judged of me. Although I do not know whether the image is that of a person who feeds it, or a person that goes on walks with it, or it is just "some human," there is a version of me that the dog sees.

We need to see how we are inside the minds of others. And we need to make sure to have a positive version of ourselves inside the minds of others. What then must we do so that a positive version of ourselves is inside others? Will this happen if we say, "Hey, you should see me positively!"? If we do this, we will likely be inside their minds more negatively. On the contrary, in order for us to go inside the minds of others in a positive manner, they must think the following when they see us: "Ah! It's nice to have this person around us." For example, just because I tell the nurse I work with, "you should respect me," does not mean she will respect me. I would have to do something worthy of her respect to earn it. If a positive version of us is in the minds of others, we will be safe wherever we go. On the other hand, if a negative version of us is in their minds, it would not be safe. I think of this as a sort of minefield. If you meddle with it in the wrong way, it will one day explode.

In the Korean TV drama "Taejo Wanggeon," at first the monk Gungye takes care of the sick by sucking out their pus and did a lot of good things, which leads many people to follow him. However, after he becomes the king, he starts drinking frequently and torments others by reading their minds. As he continues to do this, everyone eventually turns their backs on him. In this way, in order for us to be truly strong, we must help others. We need to completely fill our surroundings with our influence by helping others. We need to make sure people turn their attention and listen when we say something. If they just ignore, it can make things difficult.

If we look around, there are many things we can do to help others without going through much trouble. If someone asks me a question, I give them a thorough answer. People who hear my thorough explanations are always thankful. Giving good directions to someone who is lost on the road is one easy way to help others. We need to get to know the joy in helping others. As beings who coexist, we actually have no choice but to live by helping each other. Living in this way is riding the waves of the world according to the laws of nature. This is in the way the world works, and we need to understand this well.

To sum it up, while we are together with other living beings, we must continuously look for things that are good for ourselves and for others, whatever they may be. For couples, people need to continuously look for things that are good for themselves and their partner. For parent–child relationship, people need to look for things that are good for themselves and their children. And what is important here in all of this is empathy, which I will discuss further later on.

Finding Things that Are Good for Us and Others

Up to this point, when the things we want and what others want were in conflict with each other, we would either feel kind of bad, or we would develop feelings of resentment towards others, or our relationship with others would fall apart. But if we understand and follow the way of the world that I have been discussing so far, we will start to find reasonable actions when our desires come into conflict with others. In other words, we will look clearly into the minds of others and find things that are good for both ourselves and others. This is an important transformation in the mind.

In order to do this, we need to practice. We would be able to see others' minds clearly if we obtain the supernatural ability to read other people's minds as explained in Buddhism, but since we do not have such an ability, we have to spend a lot of time practicing getting close to others' minds. For example, if there was a person who made us uncomfortable, we would try bringing a recent image of that person to mind when we have a moment during the day by ourselves. Sometimes certain feelings may arise when we do this. If this happens, we should take note of this, stop those feelings, and keep bringing up that person's image. At other times, we may also have certain thoughts. If this happens, we should stop them and again continue to bring up an image of that person. We can get closer to someone if we can continuously contemplate them while preventing our reactions or judgments about them from arising.

The biggest obstacle when we look into others is ourselves. Due to our very old habits, we judge others with our thoughts. We need to let go of that habit of thinking and enter the minds of others. This of course is not easy. When someone is still and does not tell us anything, would it be easy to know what is in their mind? Rather than being overwhelmed with thought, when we make an effort to observe what kind of things occur inside someone else, we will come to the conclusion that "ah, it's truly difficult to know what's in someone else's mind." The mind of someone else is a huge world that has been formed by the culmination of all of the things that person has experienced in their life. How can we easily enter that world? Despite this, up to this point we have been very easily drawing conclusions that this person is like this and that person is like that. If we stop making quick judgments and start looking attentively at others, we will become humbler.

We truly respect others when we always see them and treat them while thinking, "To me there is no one more precious than myself. Whatever I think and whatever judgment I make is natural and there is a reason for it. Likewise, to that person, he or she is the most precious. There is a reason for whatever that person thinks or for whatever judgment they make." Accepting others 100% just as we accept ourselves 100% is the beginning. If we continue to do this, then the conflicts in our life will continue to lessen.

And when this happens, we will become confident in our lives. This is because we will never feel inferior to anyone as long as we think, speak, and act not just for ourselves but from the point of view of others. Furthermore, though we may continue to do things for ourselves, because we choose to do things that are good for ourselves and others after carefully considering their point of view, we will be able to have a true dialog with others. In the past, we may have said things that only benefit ourselves. And of course they were not received well by others. However, now we will say things good for ourselves and others, and even if it is hard for others to hear those things at first, things will eventually work out. Since the mind itself has changed to one where we only think of coexisting with others, regardless of where we are or who we are with, we will be in a state where we can have a productive dialog with others. This is the state we need to be in to find truly good things.

Everything is give and take. There are no exemptions. If someone dislikes us and resists the things we do, it is because there is a reason for them to dislike us. If someone likes us and collaborates with us, it is because there is a reason for them to like us. Some of you might consider this to be too calculating. However, this is not the case. This is the way of the world. We must always remember that good causes bring about happy results and bad causes bring about unhappy results.

The Buddha's Teachings on Good in Ourselves and in Others

I said that it is natural for everyone to want to do the things they like. If this is the case, does this make us happy? Let us look into this question.

We obviously know the things that we like. However, those things may change later on. But as we change our minds about those things, we may suffer later on. This means doing something because we wanted to, but suffering later on because of it. For example, it is like when we drink a lot of alcohol because we wanted to at the time, but we regret it the next day as our body suffers. Everyone here probably had a similar experience. Therefore, it is important for us to not have to change our minds.

How can we make it so that we do not have to change our minds? We have to see clearly. We can always change our minds towards things we did not see correctly, but we will not change our mind towards things we have seen clearly. Therefore, practicing to see clearly can become a path to eliminate suffering. We must also see things that are good for us and others from a broad perspective. For example, let us say that we need some money and our friend also needs some money. And so, the two of us agree to rob a bank and go through with it. Though we may immediately feel good from obtaining money, there are "others" that are involved here. These others will fight back. Among these other people, there would also be the police. Though we may have felt good about robbing the bank for a moment, let us say that we were eventually caught by the police. If that happens, the two of us will now resent each other. We may think: "We're in this mess because you said we should rob the bank. Why did you tempt me into it? You should take responsibility for my life."

Things that are good for us and others must be so when seen in the long term. Things that may be helpful temporarily but could change in the future are troublesome. We therefore need to have a lot of wisdom to see clearly.

There is a scene in the scriptures where the Buddha talks about the kinds of things that are good for us and for others in this present life and in the next life. Let us take a look.

Ambalaṭṭhikārāhulovāda Sutta (MN 61)

"What do you think, Rāhula? What is the purpose of a mirror?"

"For the purpose of reflection, venerable sir."

"So too, Rāhula, an action with the body should be done after repeated reflection; an action by speech should be done after repeated reflection, an action by mind should be done after repeated reflection."

"Rāhula, when you wish to do an action with the body, you should reflect upon that same bodily action thus:

'Would this action that I wish to do with the body lead to my own affliction, or to the affliction of others, or to the affliction of both? Is it an unwholesome bodily action with painful consequences, with painful results?'

> When you reflect, if you know: 'This action that I wish to do with the body would lead to my own affliction, or to the affliction of others, or to the affliction of both; it is an unwholesome bodily action with painful consequences, with painful results,' then you definitely should not do such an action with the body.
>
> But when you reflect, if you know: 'This action that I wish to do with the body would not lead to my own affliction, or to the affliction of others, or to the affliction of both; it is a wholesome bodily action with pleasant consequences, with pleasant results,' then you may do such an action with the body."
>
> "Also, Rāhula, while you are doing an action with the body, you should reflect upon that same bodily action thus:
>
> 'Does this action that I am doing with the body lead to my own affliction, or to the affliction of others, or to the affliction of both? Is it an unwholesome bodily action with painful consequences, with painful results?'
>
> When you reflect, if you know: 'This action that I am doing with the body leads to my own affliction, or to the affliction of others, or to the affliction of both; it is an unwholesome bodily action with painful consequences, with painful results,' then you should suspend such a bodily reaction.
>
> But when you reflect, if you know: 'This action that I am doing with the body does not lead to my own affliction, or to the affliction of others, or to the affliction of both; it is a wholesome bodily action with pleasant consequences, with pleasant results,' then you may continue with such a bodily action."
>
> "Also, Rāhula, after you have done an action with the body, you should reflect upon that same bodily action thus:
>
> 'Did this action that I did with the body lead to my own affliction, or to the affliction of others, or to the affliction of both? Was it an unwholesome bodily action with painful consequences, with painful results?
>
> When you reflect, if you know: 'This action that I did with the body led to my own affliction, or to the affliction of others, or to the affliction of both; it was an unwholesome bodily action with painful consequences, with painful results,' then you should confess such a bodily action, reveal it, and lay it open to the Teacher or to your wise companions in the holy life. Having confessed it, revealed it, and laid it open, you should undertake restraint for the future.
>
> But when you reflect, if you know: 'This action that I did with the body did not lead to my own affliction, or to the affliction of others, or to the affliction of both; it was a wholesome bodily action with pleasant consequences, with pleasant results,' then you may abide happy and glad, training day and night in wholesome states." [1]

For context, in this discourse the Buddha is giving a teaching to his ordained son Rāhula. When Rāhula was 7 years old, he kept on telling lies and so the Buddha sat him down and spoke to him using a simile of a water vessel. He tells him that the practice of a recluse who tells lies is hollow and empty like a water vessel that been turned upside down.

The passage that we have just seen is what comes afterwards. Here, the Buddha tells Rāhula that after he reflects on the actions of the body, if that action will be harmful to himself, to others, or to both (in the future), is harmful (in the present), or was harmful (in the past), it is an unwholesome action that will bring about painful results, and that they must be stopped. On the other hand, the Buddha tells Rāhula that if that action will not be harmful to himself, to others, or to both (in the future), is not harmful (in the present), or was not harmful (in the past), it is a wholesome action that will bring about pleasant results, and that he should continue to do them. Here, we can understand the effects as applying to both this present life and the next life.

Additionally, he says for unwholesome actions that have already been committed that one "should confess such a bodily action, reveal it, and lay it open to the teacher or to one's wise companions in the holy life. Having confessed it, revealed it, and laid it open, one should undertake restraint for the future." What this means is that after going to such people and confessing that "I have committed such an unwholesome action," the person should request that they reprimand him or her appropriately. Since it can be hard to avoid doing such actions when we are by ourselves, we can create a system of avoiding such things by bringing them forward to a group of people.

The Buddha continues his discourse by saying the same thing for actions that are done by speech and by the mind. Normally, we reflect on the actions we perform with our bodies and through our speech, but here the Buddha is saying we should thoroughly reflect all the way through actions performed by the mind. Therefore, Buddhism teaches us to create three kinds of wholesome karma for the body, speech, and mind.

Let us look at how this discourse concludes.

> "Rāhula, whatever recluses and brahmins in the past purified their bodily action, their verbal action, and their mental action, all did so by repeatedly reflecting thus.
>
> Whatever recluses and brahmins in the future will purify their bodily action, their verbal action, and their mental action, all will do so by repeatedly reflecting thus.
>
> Whatever recluses and brahmins in the present are purifying their bodily action, their verbal action, and their mental action, all are doing so by repeatedly reflecting thus.
>
> Therefore, Rāhula, you should train thus: 'We will purify our bodily action, our verbal action, and our mental action by repeatedly reflecting upon them.'"
>
> That is what the Blessed One said. The venerable Rāhula was satisfied and delighted in the Blessed One's words. [2]

This teaching of the Buddha was not just meant for Rāhula. It can help us in the same way. I recommend that you memorize this passage. We are beings that are affected by the things that are inside our minds. The things inside our minds are "us." By memorizing this passage to the point where if someone asks, we can say "Rāhula kept telling lies when he was 7 years old and so the Buddha gave him this teaching." we may be able to discover how much we have changed from before.

Now let us look at an example of a concrete action. Here too I will present the discourse directly. It is a scene where brahmin householders of Veḷudvāreyya approach the Buddha when he travels there and ask him to teach, to which he responds.

The People of Bamboo Gate: Veḷudvāreyya Sutta (SN 55.7)

> "Master Gotama, we have such wishes, desires, and hopes as these: 'May we dwell in a home crowded with children! May we enjoy Kāsian sandalwood! May we wear garlands, scents, and unguents! May we receive gold and silver! With the breakup of the body, after death, may we be reborn in a good destination, in a heavenly world!'
>
> As we have such wishes, desires, and hopes, let Master Gotama teach us the Dhamma in such a way that we might dwell in a home crowded with children. That we might wear garlands, scents, and unguents. That we might receive gold and silver. That with the breakup of the body, after death, we might be reborn in a good destination, in a heavenly world."
>
> "I will teach you, householders, a Dhamma exposition applicable to oneself. Listen to that and attend closely, I will speak."
>
> "Yes, sir," those brahmin householders of Bamboo Gate replied. The Blessed One said this:
>
> "What, householders, is the Dhamma exposition applicable to oneself?"
>
> "Here, householders, a noble disciple reflects thus: 'I am one who wishes to live, who does not wish to die; I desire happiness and I am averse to suffering. Since I am one who wishes to live, who does not wish to die, and am averse to suffering, if someone were to take my life, that would not be pleasing and agreeable to me. Now if I were to take the life of another—of one who wishes to live, who does not wish to die, who desires happiness and is averse to suffering—that would not be pleasing and agreeable to the other either. What is displeasing and disagreeable to me is displeasing and disagreeable to the other too. How can I inflict upon another what is displeasing and disagreeable to me?'
>
> Having reflected thus, he himself abstains from the destruction of life, exhorts others to abstain from the destruction of life, and speaks in praise of abstinence from the destruction of life. Thus this bodily conduct of his is purified in three respects." [3]

After the Buddha explains that abstaining from killing living beings is the path to happiness, he explains in the same way that not taking what is not given, not committing adultery, remaining faithful to one's wife, speaking the truth, not speaking divisively, not speaking harshly, and not speaking frivolously is the path to happiness.

We must be committed to the principle that "searching for the way that we can coexist with others is a path leading to happiness." Next, it is important to apply this appropriately to the various situations we come across while living our lives. In order to do this well however, we need to increase our wisdom. One path I recommend to increase wisdom is to read a lot of Buddhist scriptures. Though there are some teachings of the Buddha that are very subtle and hard to understand, there are also a lot of teachings that are very logical like the discourse we have just seen. The Buddha gave a variety of teachings that were all appropriate to the people who requested his help. The greatest power is in the scriptures. It is good to consistently read the scriptures so that they come up in your minds even when you are not doing anything.

Five Things We Should Have When Talking

If we look at the Pāsādika Sutta in the Dīgha Nikāya (DN 29), the Buddha explains the five things we should have when talking. Let us look at the discourse.

Pāsādika Sutta (The Delightful Discourse) (DN29)

> Cunda, if "the past" refers to what is not factual, to fables, to what is not of advantage, the Tathāgata makes no reply. If it refers to what is factual, not fabulous, but which is not of advantage, the Tathāgata makes no reply. But if "the past" refers to what is factual, not fabulous, and which is of advantage, then the Tathāgata knows the right time to reply. If "the future" refers to what is not factual, to fables, to what is not of advantage, the Tathāgata makes no reply. If it refers to what is factual, not fabulous, but which is not of advantage, the Tathāgata makes no reply. But if "the future" refers to what is factual, not fabulous, and which is of advantage, then the Tathāgata knows the right time to reply. If "the present" refers to what is not factual, to fables, to what is not of advantage, the Tathāgata makes no reply. If it refers to what is factual, not fabulous, but which is not of advantage, the Tathāgata makes no reply. But if "the present" refers to what is factual, not fabulous, and which is of advantage, then the Tathāgata knows the right time to reply. Therefore, Cunda, the Tathāgata is called the one who declares the time, the fact, the advantage, the Dhamma and the discipline. That is why he is called Tathāgata.

When speaking, truth is the starting point. We can say that the basis of Buddhist human relations is taking the truth as the basis and finding the path that will be truly helpful for other people. This is also the same in psychotherapy. We need to enter into relationships with our patients based on the truth.

So, what does the truth mean here? The truth is what you have directly seen and heard. We need to speak only as much as we have seen and heard. However, this is easier said than done. It is not only hard to clearly distinguish the things that we have directly seen and heard, but as we speak, we have a habit of unknowingly exposing our thoughts as the truth. This is why we need to carefully observe what we are saying while we are talking.

The second thing that speech should have is "rightness." The Buddha expresses this as "speech that is right or wrong," but I feel it is ok to change it slightly to "whether something is worth saying or not."

The third thing that speech should have is "benefit." The Buddha says to only speak when what we say helps others.

The fourth thing that speech should have is "timing." In this case, when is the appropriate timing? The best timing for speaking is when a question arises in the listener, or in other words when the person we are talking to asks us something. This is because when they do this, they really want to listen. Of course, even if the person does not directly ask a question, if we observe carefully, we will be able to notice that "Ah, this person is curious about this now!" When this happens, we need to say what is necessary. Freud also said something similar. He said that after the therapist gets a clear understanding of the patient, they should not just throw things back at them but rather should find the appropriate time when those things will be helpful to the patient. This means that we need to find the timing where we can maximize the effectiveness of the treatment while minimizing side effects.

The last and fifth thing that speech should have is "appropriate expression." Though this does not appear directly in the discourse above, appropriate expression is an element that cannot be left out. No matter how much of what we say is based on the truth, is valuable, helps others, and is done at the appropriate timing, if we express it in an untactful way, the person we are talking to may resist it. As much as possible, we should speak smoothly and mildly so that the person we are talking to does not resist it.

Practicing Empathy

Earlier I briefly mentioned the importance of empathy and how to cultivate the ability to empathize. Here we will take another look at this.

Empathy is knowing exactly what is in someone else's mind. For a therapist, cultivating the ability to empathize is more important than anything else. This is because we need to understand the minds of the people we face and respond accordingly. Not doing this and doing whatever we want is not very helpful to the patient. Even finding the appropriate timing to help a patient is only possible when we practice empathy and clearly understand the people we are treating. We must always go into the minds of others and understand them at a subtle level. Of course, we should not do this so much that we become oversensitive and exhausted.

In English, empathy is sometimes expressed as "walking a mile in another's shoes." Try and imagine walking someone else's shoes that do not even fit you. This is a difficult task that requires patience and effort. As I have said earlier, unless we acquire the supernatural ability to read other people's minds, we cannot clearly know what is in their minds. Actually, most of us are trying to know what is in other people's minds as they are.

To be good at empathy, we need to observe a lot of people on a regular basis. And we need to observe them in detail, whether they are children or adults. As we carefully observe why some people are well off while others are not, why some people go through divorce while others live happily in marriage, how people have abilities that we do not possess, and so on, our ability to empathize will improve.

While this may not work well at first, if we do this for a long time, we will get closer to other people's minds. This means that when we see someone, we stop having our own thoughts about them and will go into their minds. And when we know what other people truly want, we will set the foundation where we can do what is good for ourselves and others.

I have made it a goal for myself to develop the ability to empathize and have been practicing empathy for a long time. During the peak of my practice of empathy, I would even quietly observe others when riding the subway and really try to look into their minds. Looking closely at the clothes they wore, the shoes they had on their feet, the things they were carrying, etc., I would try to figure out "What kind of mind led them to that choice? What is in their minds right now?"

From the time I opened my clinic in 1990 to now, whenever a patient comes I make an effort to stop myself and enter their minds. This means stopping myself and being one with the patient. While doing this, I make comments to the patient. I found this very effective for the patient because there are often hints in the things that a patient says to me. They end up saying, "For some strange reason I don't listen to people very well outside, but here I am listening to what you're telling me." The patient listens because I am able to become one with them through their mind and speak from the inner voice inside of them. In other words, they listen because they know that it will be beneficial to them.

Actually, it is the other person who confirms whether or not I am being empathetic to them. This is because only the other person can know their own minds. And so if the other person does not react at all and remains silent, there is no way of knowing what is on their minds. Itis actually better for them to get angry and curse since this tells us about their minds.

As we practice trying to be empathetic, a few supplemental effects will arise. First, as we have looked into earlier, we will come to realize that it is hard to know the minds of others. The mind of another is a vast world that is difficult for us to enter. Once we realize this, we will stop rushing to conclusions about others' minds and will try to sincerely approach others. This realization is the biggest gain.

Secondly, we will begin to be grateful. In the end, what tells us about others' minds are their words. Nothing is better for someone who is trying to be empathetic than when someone tells us their mind through their words. Even if what they are saying is criticizing us, we will come to accept this with gratitude as it tells us "Ah, that's what this person's mind is like."

Third, we will become accepted by others as a good person. To know someone's mind, we have to listen to them well. If we do this, how will we come across in the eyes of others? Would not they think, "Hey, that person is really listening to what I am saying. They really respect me."

The Neurobiology of Empathy

There is a neuron associated with empathy. It is called a mirror neuron, discovered around the late 1990s by Italian neurophysiologist Giacomo Rizzolatti and his colleagues. After researchers attached electrodes to a monkey's brain, they researched what part of the brain reacts when the monkey grabs an object. As a result of their research, they discovered that there was a specific part of the brain that was connected to the act of grasping. But they observed that this did not just occur when the monkey grabbed an object directly, but that there was also a reaction in that part of the brain when the monkey saw another monkey grabbing an object. Thus, the mirror neuron was discovered. After this discovery, subsequent research led to the discovery that humans also had the mirror neuron.

The mirror neuron is a brain cell that performs a particular function. For example, when I look at an action performed by someone else, the action is replayed as it is within the mirror neuron. As a result, I am able to clearly know what that person is doing. In other words, a virtual simulation of the person's action occurs in the mirror neuron, allowing it to be experienced vividly as if I were doing that action myself. Through this, I am able to determine the intention contained in that action. Through this, we are able to imitate the actions of others. In his book, *The Tell-Tale*

Brain, well-known neuroscientist V.S. Ramachandran says that language and culture of human beings probably came from the function of the mirror neuron. Language evolved through imitating others' lip and tongue motions, and through this it became possible for cultural accumulation.

However, the experience through the mirror neuron is not the same as the other person's experience. This is because it functions through the inhibition circuit in the frontal lobe. For example, when we look at someone experiencing the feeling of heat when boiling water splashes on their hand, we know what kind of experience they are having, but we are not able to feel that same sensation of heat. In order to experience heat, signals that the hand is hot must be sent to the brain. However, this signal is not sent to the brain from the hand of the person that we are just looking at. In other words, it is not the heat actually occurring that is sent to the brain but rather signals. According to Ramachandran, situations where the mirror neuron is activated but there is no touch signal are interpreted by the brain as follows: "Empathize by whatever means possible. But don't feel the other person's sensations literally."

And so this means that we are able to understand and empathize with the experiences of others through the function of the mirror neuron. Additionally, the brain is not a fixed entity but rather continuously changes. According to some research, it was observed that just like during early childhood and adolescence, experiences change the neural circuits responsible for processes such as memory, emotion, and self-awareness during adulthood as well. What this means is that if we try to understand others well and observe them in detail, the mirror neuron will continue to activate and our brains will transform to better be able to empathize with others. On the other hand, if we live without paying attention to others, the number of times the mirror neuron activates will decrease and our ability to empathize will decline accordingly. For reference, according to recent research, it is said that the mirror neuron is not well developed in people who have autism.

The Path to Being One in Mind

Drawing from the saying "couples are one in body and spirit," Professor Rhee Dongshick once said "couples are two minds with different bodies." He sees that the path to harmony is to acknowledge that two people's bodies and minds are different from each other and to therefore empathize with the other's situation.

But is empathy the best thing we can do? What would happen if we could go beyond empathy and make our minds one with others? All of the tensions and difficulties that come when there are two minds would completely disappear. Though it is impossible to be one with others in body, it is possible to be one with others in mind. An example of this appears in Buddhist scriptures. Let us take a look.

The Shorter Discourse on Gosinga (Cūḷagosinga Sutta: MN 31)

The venerable Anuruddha, the venerable Nandiya, and the venerable Kimbila went to meet the Blessed One. One took his bowl and outer robe, one prepared a seat, and one set out water for washing the feet. The Blessed One sat down on the seat made ready and washed his feet. Then those three venerable ones paid homage to the Blessed One and sat down at one side. When they were seated, the Blessed One said to them:

> "I hope you are keeping well, Anuruddha, I hope you are all comfortable, I hope you are not having any trouble getting alms food."
>
> "We are all keeping well, Blessed One, we are comfortable, and we are not having any trouble getting alms food."
>
> "I hope Anuruddha, that you are all living in concord, with mutual appreciation, without disputing, blending like milk and water, viewing each other with kindly eyes."
>
> "Surely, venerable sir, we are living in concord, with mutual appreciation, without disputing, blending like milk and water, viewing each other with kindly eyes."
>
> "But, Anuruddha, how do you live in concord, with mutual appreciation, without disputing, blending like milk and water, viewing each other with kindly eyes?"
>
> "Venerable sir, as to that, I think thus: 'It is a gain for me, it is a great gain for me, that I am living with such companions in the holy life.' I maintain bodily acts of loving-kindness towards those venerable ones both openly and privately; I maintain verbal acts of loving-kindness towards them both openly and privately; I maintain mental acts of loving-kindness towards them both openly and privately. I consider: 'Why should I not set aside what I wish to do and do what these venerable ones wish to do?' Then I set aside what I wish to do and do what these venerable ones wish to do. We are different in body, venerable sir, but one in mind."
>
> The venerable Nandiya and the venerable Kimbila each spoke likewise, adding:
>
> "Venerable sir, as to that, I think thus... We are different in body, venerable sir, but one in mind.
>
> That is how, venerable sir, we are living in concord, with mutual appreciation, without disputing, blending like milk and water, viewing each other with kindly eyes." [4]

If we possess the wisdom to see that being with others is beneficial to ourselves, it is easier to attain loving kindness and "oneness in mind." But often we are in situations where we are in small or large conflicts with others, and by arousing harmful thoughts, we fall into a state where we make our own minds miserable. But what would happen if the mind of seeing and treating others with loving kindness came up first in those situations? Rather than getting angry, we would try to achieve harmony by resolving the problem. Therefore, just as much as having the wisdom to see the benefits of this, we have a realistic need to also cultivate our minds to see and treat others with loving kindness. In this case, what do we have to do in order to cultivate and maintain a mind of loving kindness?

Cultivating Four Kinds of Broad Mind

Within Buddhist practice is meditation on the Four Immeasurables. It is the practice of taking someone else as one's object and cultivating the four most open and broad minds, namely loving kindness, compassion, sympathetic joy, and equanimity. When these four kinds of mind are developed, you will have no difficulties living in this world.

We are constantly at odds with others because of our narrow mindset. But we still have to continue to be in contact with others in order to survive. And so, we inevitably suffer. But if our mindset is broad, we will have no difficulties no matter who we encounter. Our lives become easier as we are able to understand and let things go even if it is something worth coming into conflict with. When we look at it a certain way, Buddhist psychotherapy is the process of transforming a mind system which makes life difficult into a mind system which makes life easy. Therefore, developing the Four Immeasurables is an important component in Buddhist psychotherapy.

The Four Immeasurables are among the 40 objects of meditation in Samatha meditation. While I cultivated the Four Immeasurables during my practice of Samatha meditation, I had direct experience with not being hindered by anything due to the mind being filled with loving kindness, compassion, sympathetic joy, and equanimity. And so, I thought that it would be of great help in treating patients if they could also cultivate the Four Immeasurables. Meditation on the Four Immeasurables begins with empathy, and progresses by first cultivating loving kindness, compassion, and sympathetic joy, and later on cultivating equanimity on the basis of the three other minds. Though it is standard and more beneficial to first practice Samatha meditation before practicing the Four Immeasurables, it can also be effective to practicing them after calming the mind by briefly practicing mindfulness of breathing.

Meditation on the Four Immeasurables begins by first taking four kinds of people as our object. First, we practice by taking ourselves as our object. Then, we take those we are fond of or respect. Third, we take people who we feel neutral towards, and finally fourth, we take those we dislike as our object. We practice this by bringing to mind ten people from each category aside from ourselves. As this progresses and the mind becomes impartial, not favoring any object that comes to mind, we can then proceed to the stage where we take all living beings as our object.

Among the Four Immeasurables, we practice meditation on loving kindness using the following four phrases: "may so-and-so be free from danger," "may so-and-so be free from mental suffering," "may so-and-so be free from physical suffering," "may so-and-so be well and happy." We first send loving kindness to ourselves by reciting these four phrases mentally. We can change our minds drastically even if we just mentally recite, "may I be free from danger," and think of a situation of avoiding danger. Then, we mentally recite, "may I be free from mental suffering" and try to think of a state where mental suffering has disappeared and we are calm. Third, we mentally recite, "may I be free from physical suffering," and try to think of a state where physical suffering has disappeared and we are at ease, and finally after all of these things have disappeared, we send loving kindness to ourselves by mentally reciting, "may I be well and happy." After we have practiced loving kindness meditation taking ourselves as our object, we practice loving kindness meditation taking people we are fond of or respect as our object, and then people who we feel neutral towards, and finally people we dislike.

A couple notes about the object of loving kindness meditation. First, we do not practice loving kindness meditation by taking deceased people as our object. This is because a dead person cannot receive loving kindness. And additionally, we do not initially take people of the opposite sex as our object. Later on, when the mind is in an impartial state without leaning towards any object and we are practicing loving kindness meditation towards all living beings, it is fine to include people of the opposite sex.

Secondly, we practice meditation on compassion using the phrase, "may so-and-so be free from suffering." Just like loving kindness meditation, the practice of meditation on compassion goes in order from ourselves, people we are fond of or respect, people we feel neutral towards, and people we dislike. Some tell me that it is difficult to practice meditation on compassion towards some people because they probably are not suffering. However, no one in this world is free from suffering. Though we could know immediately if we ask them, when we are not able to do that, try to bring them to mind and make your best guess. You may then be able to see what kind of suffering that person could be experiencing.

Third, meditation on sympathetic joy also has one phrase, "may so-and-so not lose what they've obtained." After making your best guess as to what our target person, the object of meditation, values most, we practice wishing that they do not lose it. If the target person values fame the most, we practice by mentally reciting, "may so-and-so not lose the fame they have acquired." Meditation on sympathetic joy likewise goes in order from ourselves, the people we are fond of or respect, the people we feel neutral towards, and the people we dislike.

Finally, after the previous three meditations have gone well, we practice meditation on equanimity on the basis of having loving kindness, compassion, and sympathetic joy towards all of our four kinds of people. Meditation on equanimity is having the mind, "though I wish for this person to be well, they are still the owners of their own karma. They must live according to their karma." This means that although we had wished them well up to now, we are now seeing them with composure standing on top of the foundations of those minds. In contrast to the other three meditations, meditation on equanimity is practiced in the order of people we feel neutral towards, ourselves, people we are fond of or respect, and people we dislike.

I will explain meditation on equanimity a bit more from the perspective of absorption meditation. This is because there is something particular about the fourth absorption (*jhāna*) that we enter through meditation on equanimity. We cultivate the first, second, and third absorptions through loving kindness meditation, and likewise through meditation on compassion and sympathetic joy. Afterwards, we cultivate the first, second, and third absorptions by taking a person we feel neutral about as our object. Afterwards, the moment that we make up our minds that 'this person is the owner of their karma. They must live according to their karma,' we enter the fourth absorption. From the state of the third absorption that we had entered through the previous meditations, as happiness disappears among happiness and concentration, the two factors of the third absorption, we enter the fourth absorption. Here we enter into a realm that is different from the fourth absorption we entered through previous methods of meditation. In other words, we are entering the fourth absorption on the basis of eliminating happiness. On the other hand, the fourth absorption that we enter in meditation on equanimity is accomplished on the basis of loving kindness, compassion, and sympathetic joy. As not only suffering, but also loving kindness, compassion, and sympathetic joy disappear, and we enter a state of balance without leaning towards any living being, we come to experience, "this is what true equanimity is!"

Hating others is not helpful to us. Also, having lots of people who are suffering is not helpful to us. When everyone around us is happy, we can finally be truly happy. Therefore, it is actually natural to be happy when others do well. When we live with this kind of mindset, all the obstacles in the world will disappear. And so, meditation on these Four Immeasurables are important. If you have lived up to this point with a different mindset, you will not be used to practicing meditation on the Four Immeasurables. However, as you practice these meditations diligently, your mind itself will change and you will come to not hate anyone. This is what it means to change the mind to a system of living easily.

References

1. Bodhi B (trans) (1995). The middle length discourses of the Buddha: a translation of the Majjhima Nikāya. Simon and Schuster, New York, pp 524–525
2. Bodhi B (trans) (1995). The middle length discourses of the Buddha: a translation of the Majjhima Nikāya. Simon and Schuster, New York, p 526
3. Bodhi B (trans) (2000). The connected discourses of the Buddha: a translation of the Saṃyutta Nikāya. Wisdom Publications, Boston, MA, p 1797
4. Bodhi B (trans) (1995). The middle length discourses of the Buddha: a translation of the Majjhima Nikāya. Simon and Schuster, New York, pp 301–302

Chapter 4
The Third Principle of Buddhist Psychotherapy: Living with Wisdom

In Buddhism, "wisdom" is knowing reality as it is. And so I sometimes call Buddhist psychotherapy "wisdom therapy." This is because Buddhism places the most importance on wisdom, and also because having the wisdom to clearly see the world as it is and then living one's life accordingly prevents problems from arising in the mind, which is also in accordance with Buddhism's basic position.

Contentment Is the Gift of Wisdom

I think Buddhism is a religion of wisdom. Right now, we are living in the age of Sakyamuni Buddha. It was after spending an incredibly long time (4 incalculable eons and a 100,000 eons) cultivating the ten perfections (pāramī) as a bodhisatta that Sakyamuni Buddha founded Buddhism as we know it today. In Early Buddhism, the ten perfections that the Buddha cultivated are generosity (dāna), morality (sīla), renunciation (nekkhamma), wisdom (paññā), energy (viriya), patience (khanti), truthfulness (sacca), determination (adhiṭṭhāna), loving kindness (mettā), and equanimity (upekkhā). Among these ten perfections, wisdom is the most important. If we look at the Jātakas, scriptures which contain stories of the Buddha's past lives, the Buddha commits everything to cultivate wisdom. Whether he gives out of generosity or practices patience, he does so on the basis of wisdom. Only when he is wise is he able to do this.

Buddhism also places a lot of importance on contentment. If we look at the scriptures, the Buddha speaks often about contentment. A question arises here. "Contentment" and "discontentment" are things that are spoken about in our normal lives. Why then does the Buddha speak about contentment as a virtue that practitioners must possess? This is because contentment arises when one is wise. If we clearly look at a certain phenomenon as it is according to the law of cause and effect, we will see that the things that we possess have come about through an

H. Jeon, *Buddhist Psychotherapy*, https://doi.org/10.1007/978-3-030-63098-0_4

inevitable process that could not have been otherwise. The reason why we possess these things is because of incredible things that have happened which can be seen as nothing less than "miracles." People who have wisdom know that reality is such and live in contentment valuing the things that they possess. On the other hand, people who are not able to see this do not know how precious their possessions are. If we look at people who are not satisfied with their lives, usually they take the things that they possess for granted. And then they fixate on the things that they do not possess. And so they have no choice but to be surrounded by discontentment.

In Buddhism, "wisdom" is knowing reality as it is. And so, as I have already said before, I sometimes call Buddhist psychotherapy "wisdom therapy." This is because Buddhism places the most importance on wisdom and also because having the wisdom to clearly see the world as it is and then living accordingly prevents problems from arising in the mind, which is also in accordance with Buddhism's basic position. We will suffer to the extent that our thoughts about the world differ from the real world. And if something goes wrong while trying to resolve this suffering, problems arise in our mental health. The basis of Buddhist psychotherapy is helping people who are suffering from these problems to open the eye of wisdom so that they can live in accordance with nature.

Three Obstacles that Prevent Us from Seeing Reality

Thoughts often differ from reality. And so we need to let go of our thoughts and continue to practice seeing reality. If after seeing the result of our actions, we think that when the result is good, we have seen something close to reality, while if the result is bad, we have failed to see reality, it is almost always right.

In order for seeing to be established, there needs to be the subject which sees and the object which is seen. However, there are three obstacles that get between the subject and object and prevent us from clearly seeing the object. If we do not eliminate those obstacles, we will be unable to properly see reality.

The first is our own life history. The past which we have experienced and lived can distort our vision and prevent us from seeing reality. For example, if we are caught up with something in our minds, we will see the world that way. People with an educational complex will be preoccupied with education when seeing the world, and those who are caught up with money will be preoccupied with money when they see the world. As a result, they will see a world that is distorted by their preoccupation with academics or money. Aside from such preoccupations, even things such as a small intention can also distort reality. For example, if there is a persistent question in our minds that too can prevent us from seeing reality as it is. Therefore, we must make sure that we are not caught up in anything within ourselves. This is because it can be the reason for distortion to arise. We must not be caught up in our own life history.

The second obstacle is culture. Just as individual people have personalities, there are things that people from a particular region share in common, and this is culture.

Culture is left behind by our ancestors or the natural environment, and we come to see the world under its influence. For example, let us say that there is a society that has the culture of premarital chastity. People who live in that society will see the world under the influence of premarital chastity. And if something happens to someone related to premarital chastity, they will judge that person on the standard of premarital chastity rather than looking at their mind or their suffering.

The third obstacle is the limitations of being human. As humans, we possess a body and a mind. And the body has sense organs such as the eyes or the brain. We see the world through these sense organs, things can get distorted in that process. There may be limitations in the ability of a sense organ to perceive an object. The sense organ's function may also be limited by the state it is or the brain is in. Also, as human beings everyone wants to be happy; no one wants to suffer. We want the things we like, not the things we do not like. We want to survive, not die. These desires can cause distortion.

However, there is hope for eliminating these three obstacles. These obstacles arise as mental functions such as our thoughts, emotions, or values. Therefore, all we have to do is be aware of them when they arise and stop them. This becomes possible when we strengthen our ability to observe by consistently training ourselves to see our mental functions. When obstacles begin to arise in our minds, we can stop them immediately and make an effort to see reality. Through such training, we can get closer and closer to reality. And so, now we must carefully observe the things that arise within ourselves to escape from the influence of our thoughts, emotions, and values.

Focusing on the Present

Focusing on the present is extremely important. We need to make an effort to focus on the mind and body and be aware of the things that arise moment to moment. In my opinion, this is the best practice and the best method for mental health.

Among my patients, especially those who suffer from bipolar disorder or psychosis, there are those who ask what they can do to stop taking medicine. I tell them the following: "There is a way to stop. You can stop taking medicine when things improve and you are able to immediately be aware of the phenomena that arise in your mind moment to moment, and if you are able to let go of harmful things that arise all day." This is the truth.

What I mean is that because we are not able to see ourselves moment to moment, we begin doing things that are harmful to our mental health. Even if these things are not strong moment to moment, if they accumulate over not just a day or 2 but over several months or several years, they will become too strong to deal with. However, if we deal with these things that are not helpful to our mental health as they arise moment to moment, they will become weak and easy to deal with.

And so we should all focus on the body and mind from the moment we open our eyes in the morning to the moment we fall asleep at night so that we can be immediately be aware of whatever phenomenon arises and attain the ability to stop the things that are harmful to ourselves. Once this is well established, we can help clients or patients who come to us to be able to do that too.

Three Things that Poison the Mind

As I have stressed repeatedly, we need to have wisdom to protect ourselves as we live our lives and to do the things that are truly helpful to us. If we do not have wisdom, we will continue to do things that are harmful to us. What exactly are the things that are harmful to us? Anything that has as its basis the three poisons of greed, hatred, and ignorance discussed in Buddhism, or that arouses them is harmful.

There are some things that I lament about psychoanalysis of the West. Western psychoanalysis is not aware of the "cognitive process" that is dealt with in Buddhism. And so when one of the three poisons arises, Western psychoanalysis is unable to clearly see what kind of effect it has on our minds. Psychoanalysis places a lot of importance on "repression." For example, they say that if you repress anger when it arises, it can explode later on. They therefore suggest that you express it in an acceptable way. Of course, it is much better to be angry once and get over it than to continue to possess that anger. However, it is important to know the fact that such anger can have an incredible effect on us. Being unaware of this can be rather troublesome.

Within the cognitive process there is something called "javanas." It arises seven times as consciousness after an object has been determined by the mind. If we become angry, even if it is only for a brief moment, the chain of cognitive processes will arise hundreds of billions of times per second. The javanas that arise within this cognitive process affect the entire body and are all connected with one's karma. If we can see such subtle things, we will know with certainty how dangerous anger is. And so the Buddha went to the extreme when speaking of anger, saying that those who become angry are not his disciples. He said to not get angry even if someone is cutting you with a saw.

When we talk about anger, usually we only consider things that are expressed externally as anger. However, there is more to be angry than this. In fact, restraining ourselves is also part of anger. Rejecting is anger. We become angry if our minds are not at ease through understanding and acceptance. Of course, there are various degrees of anger. There is a difference between scowling and yelling out of anger and restraining ourselves.

Let us take a moment here to talk in more detail about the three poisons. First, ignorance is not knowing the law of karma or in other words, the law of cause and effect. If someone commits a wrongdoing, then that person will receive all of that action's effects. This means that if someone harms others, they will receive much more harm in return. Likewise, if we help or give to others, we will receive many times the benefit in return. Seeing this principle clearly is not being ignorant. But because we are not able to see this, greed and anger arises on the basis of ignorance.

Greed is clinging onto things that follow the laws of cause and effect, and anger is pushing away things that follow the laws of cause and effect. In other words, things simply arise because they are supposed to, but unaware of this, we cling onto them or push them away.

Whenever I talk about the law of karma, there is a counterargument that I always get. This is that when we look at the world, there are bad people who are living well. It may seem like this from the outside. However, this is not actually the case. If we do something that is bad, then we will definitely receive something many times as bad in return. But it is difficult to see this truth of karma properly unless we are at the level of the Buddha. This is because the things that make up the world are connected in a manner that is far too complicated.

In "The Discourse on Inconceivable Matters" in the Aṅguttara Nikāya (AN 4.77), the Buddha speaks of four things that can drive one to madness or frustration if they think about them. The first is the domain of the Buddhas, the second is the depth of absorption (jhāna), the third is the effects of karma, and the fourth is speculation about the world (thinking about things like "how did this tree form?"). This means that trying to understand the effects of karma by just thinking about it will only cause us headaches. And so we must have faith in the law of karma. Though I have been able to see a little into karma through my practice, I still rely on the Buddha's teachings in terms of karma. Most of us will have to approach karma through faith.

We must be extremely careful with greed, hatred, and ignorance. This is because when these things accumulate, they become the basis for bad mental health, and many mental problems arise on the basis of these three poisons. And so in order for there to be genuine, fundamental treatment, we must make it so that the mind operates without greed, hatred, and ignorance. We do not necessarily need an incredible amount of wisdom to achieve this. If we just focus on the present, greed, hatred, and ignorance will be absent in that moment. We can say that if we focus on the present all day, beneficial cognitive functions will continue to arise.

The Importance of Seeing Clearly

We must be able to see clearly. When something happens, we need to clearly see how it affects us. However, it seems that many people do not do this. For example, some people who do not invest in the stock market become happy when stock prices fall. However, falling stock prices could mean that the economy is not doing well. This effect can extend all the way to the people who do not invest and can also make their circumstances worse.

There is a story that I often tell related to this. Let us say that the best guitarist in our country is guitarist A. When A performs, people flock together and look for A everywhere. But then one day, a superstar B who is incredible at playing guitar appears, and everyone starts cheering for B. This makes A think, "Ah, it looks like my time is over. It'll be a difficult road ahead." However, reality may be different from what A is thinking. The popularity of guitarists as a whole may increase even more with the appearance of B, and at the same time people who liked A's music may continue to do so. Also, A may be able to further develop their own music by watching how B acquired such skill. In other situations, B might have problems and fade away quickly, allowing A to reemerge. There is no way of knowing for sure what will happen. And so we must not react emotionally, but clearly see what has happened and continue to do the things we should be doing.

There is a proverb, "an envious man waxes lean with the fatness of his neighbor." But if we look at the reality of the situation, if our neighbor does well, we may get invited to dinner. We do well when others do well. Among my high school alumni, I had a friend who would be happy when others did well as if he was doing well. This is an example of someone who sees things clearly My friend understood that if the other alumni do well, good things will happen to him as well. At the very least he would be able to get a drink, and if the alumni association is well funded, all the alumni may be able to go on vacation together.

As I have said previously, the most beneficial thing for us is to live according to the Four Immeasurables. If we live with the mindset of loving kindness, compassion, sympathetic joy, and equanimity, the obstacles in our minds will disappear and we will be able to live very easily. Among the various Buddhist meditation practices, I found I was happiest when I practiced meditation on the Four Immeasurables. Broadening the mind and not being caught up in anything is an extraordinary experience.

"A Beautiful Mind"

There is a film called "A Beautiful Mind." The film tells the story of John Nash, a genius mathematician whose life is in turmoil due to schizophrenia, as he overcomes his mental illness and eventually wins the Noble Prize for economics.

John Nash begins suffering from schizophrenia when he was in college. His condition continues to worsen until eventually he believes his life is in danger while working on a secret government project. However, he believes what he is seeing is real and rejects treatment, which makes his delusion continue to get more severe. He was living in extreme fear and anxiety when one day he comes to realize he was living in his own delusion. What John realized was that the young niece of a close friend whom he had known for a long time never grew older and therefore both the niece and his friend were actually fabrications of his own delusion. Afterwards John undergoes extensive treatment and eventually recovers to the point where he is able to live an almost normal life.

The turning point in John Nash's life was when he looked straight at reality and learned that what he was seeing may not be real, since a child who never ages cannot exist in reality. Towards the end of the film, there is a scene where John points to a stranger who had sought him out after class and asks the student next to him, "Do you see this person?" You can argue that by this point he is able to stay away from his illness since he has learned and put to practice a method to protect himself from his delusions.

I always tell the story of this film to people who come to my clinic suffering from psychosis because it is extremely helpful to their treatment.

Training to See Reality

In order to live with a healthy mind, we need to understand that our thoughts can differ from reality and we must train ourselves to set aside our thoughts and see reality as it is. The best thing to do when training to see reality is observing carefully the things that arise in our body and minds from the moment we open our eyes in the morning to the moment we fall asleep at night. If we observe well, we can see that what we think is often different from what actually occurs.

For example, let us look at what actually happens when we eat. Normally when we eat, we simply think that "we are eating" without really knowing what is happening. However, if we observe closely, we can see that various processes occur while we eat. We first see the food. Then we grab ahold of our silverware. Then, we take our silverware to the food and pick it up. And then we bring the silverware to our mouth, during which our mouth opens. Then we put the food into our mouth, close our mouth, chew the food while spit forms in our mouth, break down the food into small bits, and finally swallow the food which has now become pulp through our throats, where it travels to the stomach. Additionally, we can observe the processes that occur while eating in even more detail than this.

There are both things that we know and do not know. It seems that there is a tendency to mix things up that comes from our attempt to simplify complex phenomena that occur in the world so that we can deal with them effectively. And it is also true that as we live our lives, it becomes harder and harder to have the luxury of thoroughly observing reality. And so, we tend to rush through and automate the processing of information that is inputted into us while following certain patterns.

But if we consistently practice observing, the things we know and do not know will become clearer. We will know the things we do know much better, and if there is something we do not know, we will also come to know whether or not there is a way to know it clearly. And if we are not able see a way to know what is unknown, we will stop. In fact, it is extremely wise to know when we do not know something.

The mind has the "function of knowing," but if we have too many thoughts, emotions, or preconceived notions, this function of knowing will not be able to operate at its full capacity. The mind's function of knowing operates fully when we enter absorption, especially the fourth absorption. In the state of the first absorption, it is difficult for the mind's function of knowing to operate fully since initial application, sustained application, joy, and happiness remain. And of course, it is also difficult for the mind's function of knowing to operate fully in the second absorption as joy and happiness remain, and in the third absorption as happiness remains. Once we enter the fourth absorption where only equanimity and concentration remain, the mind can clearly see anything without any distraction. To express this in non-Buddhist terms, we are able to clearly see when the mind is devoid of things like thoughts, emotions, or preconceived notions, and is calm and solely focused on an object.

And so it is important to focus on the present. If we continuously focus on the present, there will be less and less room for other things to interfere, allowing us to know objects fully. If we observe the things that we do and the things that arise along with them all day, we will come to know that the body and mind are not ours. This is because if it is ours, we should be able to do with them as we please, but as I have discussed before, things such as thoughts or intentions arise when certain conditions are met, not because we want them to. We are not able to freely choose the contents of our thoughts and intentions, yet mental functions such as thoughts and intentions are always present in the things that we do every day. How then can the body and mind be ours?

If we look at the scriptures, the Buddha speaks frequently of sati and sampajañña, which refer to focusing the mind (sati) and clearly knowing (sampajañña) what is arising. In other words, when we eat, focusing on eating and clearly knowing what arises during that process is sati and sampajañña. To do this, we have to focus on the present. Reality is focusing on the present and knowing a 100% what is happening.

The Buddha's Step-by-Step Teachings

If we look at the "Gaṇakamoggallāna Sutta" in the Majjhima Nikāya (MN 107), we will find the steps of practice that one must take in their practice. While speaking to the Buddha, the accountant Gaṇaka Moggallāna asks whether there is an order to the Buddha's teachings, just as there is an order to building an auditorium, an order to learning archery, and an order to learning accounting. To this the Buddha says that just as when a skilled horse trainer obtains a thoroughbred, they first train the horse to get used to wearing a bit on their mouths before training the horse further, there is also an order to guiding practitioners. That order is as follows.

First is following the monastic code. This must be the foundation of one's practice. The monastic code is a set of rules that have been determined so that we do not do things that are harmful to the body and mind while doing the things that are helpful to the body and mind. The monastic code is not meant to be prohibitive, but rather protective. Someone who does not know what is good or bad for the body and mind will unknowingly do things that are harmful to them. And afterwards they will not even be able to practice as they will be too busy resolving their situation. Following the monastic code protects us so that the mind which has not yet been trained does not do things that are harmful.

Second is guarding the doors of one's senses. Guarding the doors of one's senses means that when we come across something, we restrain ourselves from grasping at its entire form or at its parts and features. For example, when we come across someone of the opposite sex, thinking 'this is a man' or 'this is a woman' is grasping at its entire form, and seeing things like the person's clothes or jewelry is grasping at its parts and features. Not grasping at the entire form or its parts and features means either seeing that object as it truly is (as mental and material phenomena) or seeing it a 100%. Seeing a 100% means stopping our thoughts, emotions, etc. and focusing solely on the object. If we do this, we will fully know the object. On the other hand, if we do not do this, harmful things such as greed or hatred will rush in like the tide.

Third is eating properly. Eating properly means knowing the appropriate amount of food to eat and accepting it while reflecting on it with wisdom. It is eating moderately, not for the pleasure of its taste, or to gain weight, or to improve one's physique, but to support the body and calm the mind so that we can live a life of purity. Does not it feel unpleasant when we eat too much? Avoiding this is eating properly.

Fourth is always being awake. It is protecting oneself from things that obstruct the mind by focusing the consciousness when we practice sitting or walking meditation.

Fifth is always maintaining mindfulness (sati) and clear knowledge (sampajañña). This is focusing on the present and clearly knowing what is arising throughout the day, even when we eat or put on clothes or go to the bathroom.

Finally, sixth is entering absorption. It is taking the previous five as one's foundation and entering the first through the fourth absorptions. After the Buddha spoke of these six things, he said the following to Gaṇaka Moggallāna: "This is my instruction, brahmin, to those bhikkhus who are in the higher training, whose minds have not yet attained the goal, who abide aspiring to the supreme security from bondage. But these things conduce both to a pleasant abiding here and now and to mindfulness and full awareness for those bhikkhus who are arahants with taints destroyed, who have lived the holy life, done what had to be done, laid down the burden, reached their goal, destroyed the fetters of being and are completely liberated through final knowledge" [1].

Conditional Freedom and Happiness vs. Unconditional Freedom and Happiness

If we consistently read Buddhist scriptures, we will naturally start to think that we should seek unconditional freedom and happiness rather than conditional freedom and happiness. If we attain unconditional freedom and happiness, we can be free and happy regardless of the conditions around us. Buddhism seeks this very path.

We usually delight in conditional freedom and happiness, such as the happiness that comes when we have money or when we are healthy. This kind of freedom and happiness disappears when its conditions disappear. It means that if we lose our money and become unhealthy, we will be unhappy. Actually, such conditional freedom and happiness will automatically come once their conditions are met. Though it may take some effort to fulfill those conditions, in some ways this kind of freedom and happiness is rather passive and can be accomplished by anyone.

On the other hand, we must exert active effort and require wisdom in order to attain unconditional freedom and happiness. When I talked about this during a family gathering, they had trouble understanding this. Some even said it makes no sense. However, it actually does make sense.

The reason why I talk about unconditional happiness and freedom is because it can be helpful to people if psychotherapists know this. If a therapist attains unconditional happiness and freedom and teaches it to people, those people will see the world in a different light. People tend to be stuck in preconceived notions, and so they have a hard time when they do not have things like money. However, it is possible to not have a hard time even when we do not have any money. A therapist can present this possibility to their patients.

I came to know that unconditional happiness and freedom is possible by reading Buddhist scriptures. If we look at the scriptures, there is no mention of the Buddha having a hard time due to any conditions. This is also the case for arahants. It is said that as an arahant though you may still experience physical pain, you will not experience any mental suffering. They are able to speak of unconditional happiness and freedom because they were able to live without mental suffering in any circumstance.

In the Hatthaka Sutta of the Aṅguttara Nikāya (AN 3.35), the Buddha talks about how to sleep well. In this discourse lies a hint for unconditional happiness and freedom. Let us take a look at what we need to do in order to always sleep well.

Hatthaka Sutta (AN3.35)

Thus have I heard. On one occasion, the Blessed One was dwelling at Āḷavī on a heap of [fallen] leaves spread out on a cow track in a siṃsapā grove. Then Hatthaka of Āḷavī, while walking and wandering for exercise, saw the Blessed One sitting there. He then approached the Blessed One, paid homage to him, sat down to one side, and said to the Blessed One:

"Venerable sir, did the Blessed One sleep well?"

"Yes, prince, I slept well. I am one of those in the world who sleep well."

"But, venerable sir, the winter nights are cold. It is the eight-day interval, the time when snow falls. The ground trampled by the hooves of cattle is rough, the spread of leaves is thin, the leaves on the tree are sparse, the ochre robes leave one cold, and the gale wind blows cold. Yet the Blessed One says thus: 'Yes prince, I slept well. I am one of those in the world who sleep well.'"

"Well then, prince, I will question you about this matter. You should answer as you see fit. What do you think, prince? A householder or a householder's son might have a house with a peaked roof, plastered inside and out, draft-free, with bolts fastened and shutters closed. There he might have a couch spread with rugs, blankets, and covers, with an excellent covering of antelope hide, with a canopy above and red bolsters at both ends. An oil

> lamp would be burning and his four wives would serve him in extremely agreeable ways. What do you think, would he sleep well or not, or what do you think about this?"
> "He would sleep well, venerable sir. He would be one of those in the world who sleep well."
> "What do you think, prince? Might there arise in that householder or householder's son bodily and mental fevers born of lust, which would torment him so that he would sleep badly?"
> "Yes, venerable sir."
> "There might arise in that householder or householder's son bodily and mental fevers born of lust, which would torment him so that he would sleep badly; but the Tathāgata has abandoned such lust, cut it off at the root, made it like a palm stump, obliterated it so that it is no more subject to future arising. Therefore I have slept well.
> "What do you think, prince? Might there arise in that householder or householder's son bodily and mental fevers born of hatred… bodily and mental fevers born of delusion, which would torment him so that he would sleep badly?"
> "Yes, venerable sir."
> "There might arise in that householder or householder's son bodily and mental fevers born of delusion, which would torment him so that he would sleep badly; but the Tathāgata has abandoned such delusion, cut it off at the root, made it like a palm stump, obliterated it so that it is no more subject to future arising. Therefore I have slept well." [2]

This discourse likely occurred before the official Buddhist monastic order (Saṅgha) was established. It seems like the Buddha was resting by the road, much like a homeless person in today's world. Then, the prince of that region comes and asks the Buddha if he has slept well. And in response, the Buddha says that he is someone who sleeps well.

The prince cannot understand what the Buddha said, you usually need a good bed, a reasonable temperature, and for it to be quiet to sleep well, yet the Buddha who slept on the street introduced himself as someone who sleeps well.

Here, the Buddha awakens the prince to the fact that internal conditions are more important than external conditions for sleeping well. No matter how comfortable your sleeping arrangements may be, if your mind boils with the heat of greed, hatred, and ignorance, you will not be able to sleep well. If however, you expel greed, hatred, and ignorance and extinguish their flames, you will be able to sleep well regardless of the external conditions.

After reading this passage, I started to think that if we strengthen our minds, we can prevent anything from causing us to suffer. I took this opportunity to seek out unconditional freedom and happiness. If it is something that the Buddha and his disciples could attain, we can attain it too. And this does not mean that we have to become a Buddha or even a monk or nun. Anyone can do this as long as they make the right effort.

How then can we attain unconditional freedom and happiness? I have come up with some ways to put things into practice in our lives to attain this.

Attaining Unconditional Freedom and Happiness: On Bodily Health

First, let us look into ways of attaining unconditional freedom and happiness by using the body's health as an example.

The good thing about being healthy is that we are free and happy. And so we have no problem with living when we are healthy.

The problem is when we are not healthy. People tend to think of being unhealthy as preventing them from being free or happy. Of course, it is true that there are certain discomforts that come with being unhealthy. However, this does not mean that we cannot be free or happy. We can live freely and happily even when we are not healthy. How can we do this? The method that I found was to look at the positives of being unhealthy. The positives of being unhealthy will differ depending on the person. Here are six things that I have found.

First, being ill becomes an opportunity to train ourselves to accept it. I have said several times that Buddhism speaks of the law of cause and effect. If we look at it from that point of view, there is a reason why we become ill. There was a cause that led to the result of becoming ill. Therefore when we are not healthy, we should learn to accept it while thinking, "Ah, this is something that occurred according to the law of cause and effect. There must be some reason for this." What we are doing here is training ourselves to not reject being ill but to accept it as it is. If we are able to train our minds to accept when we are ill as it is, then we will be able to accept other phenomena when they arise as they are as well.

Second, it becomes an opportunity to discover bad habits we may have that cause the body to be ill and to fix them. There is a hypnosis inducing phrase that Herbert Spiegel created to use when hypnotizing patients to stop smoking. It is as follows: "The body is like a pet. A pet eats whatever its owner gives it. Likewise, our body will eat whatever we give it. Let's take care of our body from now on. Don't give the body bad things. Smoking is bad." The body takes in what we give it and does what we tell it to do. If we eat the wrong food, our stomach will hurt, and if we are exposed to too much cold air, we will get sick. This is the way our body works. When the body is ill, it is the result of us doing something wrong. Therefore, the body's illness can be a signal indicating to us that if we will be in trouble if we continue doing what we are doing, and it can also be a signal telling us to fix it. If we follow that signal and closely examine what went wrong and we fix it, we can prevent ourselves from becoming ill from doing those wrong things. There are some people who are normally very energetic but then suddenly collapse. Their bodies were naturally strong, and so they did not become ill even though they were doing the wrong things. However, those things continued to build up until they suddenly came down hard. In some ways, it is better for us to be a little ill more often rather becoming very ill.

Third, it becomes an opportunity for us to get rest and have time to ourselves. We should rest when our body is ill. And as we rest, we will be able to have time to ourselves. Usually, sickness comes when we push ourselves too hard at work or doing other things. While we had not felt that this was a problem at the time, being sick presents us the opportunity to rest and look back at ourselves. This can also become an opportunity to change the way we live our lives.

Fourth, it becomes an opportunity for us to realize that the body is not ours, or in other words to realize the Buddhist notion of no-self (anatta). When the body is healthy, we think that it is listening to us well. We also think the same way about the mind. However, this is not the case. Patients who have sought me out are at the very least well aware that the mind is not theirs. When I tell them that the body and mind are not ours, there are a lot of people who say, "Ah, yes I know that the mind is not mine." This is because these patients constantly have experiences such as feeling depressed or having anxious thoughts even when they do not want to. Under the same principle, people whose bodies are ill will come to understand that the body does not listen to them.

The body not only does not listen to us when it is ill, but it also does not listen to us when it is healthy. The body simply functions according to its own laws following the principle of cause and effect. It is past and present conditions that continue to lead the body. This is easy to see when we are not healthy. If we are able to realize this and can maintain this knowledge even when we're healthy, then we've definitely realized no-self. The body's suffering is an opportunity for us to see the truth. Make an effort to discover this when you are ill.

Fifth, it becomes an opportunity to appreciate the things we have and to live a life where we are satisfied with what we have. When we are ill, we realize that being healthy is precious. If our bodies have become ill to the point where we can barely do things that we would normally do easily or cannot even imagine doing them, we will become keenly aware that the body's ability to simply function is precious. Just walking, just eating, just sleeping are actually miracles. It is hard to get around if we have diarrhea or an upset stomach. It is actually incredible that we can go about our lives without worrying about having to go to the bathroom. We have to be able to see such things clearly. Those who understand these truths all the time, not only when the body is ill but also when it is healthy, have somewhat of an eye for seeing reality.

Those who understand that being healthy is precious even when they are healthy are truly remarkable. Usually, we take the functions that our bodies have for granted and live in a state of discontentment focusing only on the things that we think we lack. I have mentioned this before, but contentment is something that has wisdom as its basis. This is because contentment arises when we see reality clearly. Even the Buddha points out that contentment as a virtue of a practitioner.

Sixth, it becomes an opportunity to know that life is limited, or in other words, that someday we will die. When we are healthy, we do not usually think a lot about death. It is only when we are ill that we start to clearly feel that just like this illness came upon us even though we did not want it to, death will also come upon us even if we do not want it to. And if we become really ill, all of the greedy desires we had when we were healthy suddenly fade away. We become aware of the fact that we do not know when we are going to die, and this can help us truly value our time.

These are six positive things about being ill that I have found. However, the things that one can find will depend on the person. If we find positive things about being ill and enjoy them when we are ill, and also take care of yourself when we are healthy, nothing concerning the body's health will give you a hard time. If we change our way of thinking in this way and put this knowledge into practice in our lives, we can also help others in a similar context.

Obtaining Unconditional Freedom and Happiness: On Money

This time let us look into the issue of money. Money is the same as health. When we have money, all we have to do is use it well and make our lives free, happy, and meaningful. And when we do not have money, we just have to look for the positive things about not having money and enjoy them. The way I see it, being at ease in the mind even when we do not have any money at all is being Buddhist in the right way. The Buddha and his disciples all did this.

I have in my own way found two positive things about not having much money. The first is that it can mean we have a lot of free time. To earn money, we have to do something for others since money is something that we receive as payment for doing something to others. And because we need time to do things for others, we have to spend a lot of time in order to earn a lot of money. If we look at it this way, not having a lot of money means that we did not spend as much time doing things for others, which means we have that much more of our own time. This will not always be the case since one's circumstances will vary from person to person, but this works well in many people's cases.

The most important thing in life is time. We are beings that die once we have spent all of our time, and time makes everything possible. The fact that there is a lot of such precious time is a good thing. Of course, it's a different story if we do not use that time well, for example, when some people suffer from weariness because time is not passing fast enough. Among my patients there are some who really have a lot of time, and I sometimes tell them this: "You are rich in terms of time. As rich as a large conglomerate. I on the other hand am poor in terms of time." Personally, I think it would be nice if there were a way to buy some time, but since there is currently no way to literally buy time, I cannot help but feel a bit disappointed. However, I think about time as follows: "It's good when patients come, since I can help patients and earn money. It's also good when patients don't come, since I can do what I want with my time. I just need to have enough patients so that I don't have to close my clinic."

In any case, when we do not have much money, we usually have a lot of time. Therefore, we have to find a way to use that time well. If we did not spend much time with our family, we can increase that time. If we want to get wiser, we can focus more time on reading, contemplating, and practicing meditation. If we want to take care of our bodies, we can start exercising moderately every day. And if we want to earn money, we can look into ways to earn money and take action.

The second positive thing about not having much money is that there is something we do not lose. In other words, there is something we lose when we have a lot of money. For example, there are a lot of cases where people who are very well off in terms of money end up losing interest in things in life. I still vividly remember how good the noodles that I ate in middle school were. Since I did not have much money at that time, I could not eat as well and as freely as I can these days. This may be why I thought everything I ate was delicious. However, these days people can easily find delicious food, but do not seem to enjoy it as much as before. The same is also true for traveling. In the past, traveling overseas was difficult. This is partially due to regulations countries set up in terms of travel, but also because of a lack of money. One person I knew was in commerce and traveled frequently. There were times I thought it would be nice to sneak inside his bag and travel with him. While there are still people these days who do not have the money to travel overseas, usually we are not able to go because we do not have time, while this may also vary depending on one's financial situation. And since we have reached the point where we can freely travel overseas, we are often less satisfied with traveling. If we travel often, it stops being as much fun.

In this way, there are clearly positive things about not having much money. Though these things may differ depending on the person, if we find them apply them to our lives, there is no reason that we cannot be free or happy just because we do not have money. The important thing here is changing our perspective. Thinking something is good but something else does not make things difficult. Having the state of mind to see things as good regardless of what they are is the road to unconditional freedom and happiness.

Obtaining Unconditional Freedom and Happiness: Freedom from Comparing Ourselves with Others

Comparing ourselves with others is also something that can make us unhappy. People have the habit of automatically comparing themselves to others. They look at the president and think, "Ah, I'm not as good as that person," or look at an actor and think, "why am I so unattractive," and suffer. On the other hand, they look at a beggar and think, "I'm better than that person," and feel good. In short, it is because of our habit to compare ourselves with others that we create the conditions for making ourselves happy or unhappy. Therefore, it is extremely important to get rid of comparing ourselves with others.

There are three things to comparing, namely "I am better than so-and-so" "I am worse than so-and-so" and "I am the same as so-and-so." In comparison, there is always an object. We always compare ourselves to an object. In other words, we compare because others have come into our lives. We have to work and rest according to our own needs. But if we compare ourselves with others, we will try to adjust to their views rather than our own needs, making it so that we are not able to live in a way that suits us.

When patients come, I use a wallet as a metaphor to have the following conversation about comparing.

"When you buy something, are you or not able to spend as much money as you have?"

"I am"

"Does the money in this wallet increase because others see you favorably? And on the other hand, does it decrease if they do not see you favorably?"

"No."

"We are beings that live to the extent of the knowledge we have and the state of our bodies. Whether others see us favorably or unfavorably, or whether we see ourselves above or below others doesn't change what we have. If there's something we need in life, we need to make an effort to obtain that. There is no use to just comparing ourselves with others."

If we stop comparing ourselves with others, we can be our true selves, and much of the suffering that comes from comparing will disappear. The Buddha says the following about comparing in the "Discourse on the Octad of the Supreme" in the Sutta Nipāta: "One should not take oneself as 'equal' or think of oneself as 'inferior' or 'superior'" [3]. What he is saying here is that we should live a life without comparing. The Buddha said this to mean that if we compare ourselves with others, we will sow discord with them and create suffering.

But even in the case of comparing, three conditions must be met for it to arise. This means that we compare ourselves with others because the right conditions are met. If we do not have a system of comparing established within us, it will not even arise. In that case, what are the conditions that cause comparing ourselves to others to arise? First, there is the concept of "I" and since there is an "I," it becomes the standard for which we compare ourselves to be better than, worse than, or the same as others.

Secondly, when we compare ourselves with others, we tend to take a narrow point of view of only seeing one "factor." When we compare, we most definitely do not consider everything. Rather, we take one thing from the whole to compare. For example, a person who values education will see someone and compare themselves by saying, "Ah, it must be so good for that person since they got into Seoul National University. What's wrong with me?" Though there are many other factors such as health, personality, and relationships, this person only sees "Seoul National University."

Finally, there is the narrow point of view of only seeing the "result" and not the entire process. If we continue with the preceding example, there are a lot of things one must sacrifice to get into Seoul National University. You may have to sacrifice having fun, getting sleep, and even your health. But the person who compares does not see this entire process and compares themselves only by looking at the result that is "Seoul National University."

These three conditions must be met for comparing to arise. In that case, how can we break the habit of comparing ourselves with others? The second condition that makes comparing arise, namely having the narrow point of view of only seeing one "factor," disappears if we continue to practice seeing the whole rather than just seeing the factor that is the focus of comparing. Just because we are inferior to someone in one thing doesn't mean that we are inferior in all aspects. While we may be inferior in some ways, we may be superior in others. The third condition that makes comparing arise, namely having the narrow point of view of only seeing the "result," disappears if we look at the entire process leading to that result. If we look at the entire process that someone had to undertake for more than 10 years to get into Seoul National University, there will probably be a lot of people who will say, "I couldn't have done all of that. I'm better off not having gone to Seoul National University."

However, the best way to stop comparing ourselves with others is to get rid of the notion of "I," the first condition that causes comparing to arise. If that is the case, how can we get rid of this notion of "I"? Usually, we look at others and come back to "ourselves." But rather than doing this, all we have to do is always look at others. If we always only look at others, we will stop comparing. If we look hard at others, we will acquire wisdom. We will come to know, "Ah! These results come because they've lived this way."

After observing others for a long time, I have seen that people who are having a hard time in their lives are always fixated on things like whether or not they are doing well, what their goals are in life, etc. In other words, people who are having a hard time have their attention focused solely on themselves.

In contrast, people with a healthy mind have their attention turned outward. Since they are interested in the things that happen externally rather than thinking about themselves, they do not have the suffering that comes from solely thinking about themselves. Also, when those around them do well, they look closely at how this came to be, and if others do not do well, they understand well why. And they are also able see what kinds of effects come from those people doing well and not doing well. With that they come to understand that good things happen to them when others do well, and bad things happen to them when others do not do well. Once they understand this, comparing oneself with others will have no ground to stand on. Since they always take an interest in the way the world works and have cultivated wisdom by thoroughly observing the world, living life in the world reveals itself easily. If we speak in Buddhist terms, they have acquired the ability to see things clearly as they are, allowing them to live smoothly following the law of cause and effect.

Living Wisely: 17 Paths that Lead to Good Mental Health

In addition to the three that I introduced up to this point, I have found 17 more paths that lead to good mental health. While seeing patients, I have come to learn of ways to living freely, reasonably, and wisely. In many cases, patients usually have problems in at least one of the following 17 areas.

1. **Reacting in a healthy way**

   The first is reacting in a healthy way. This means not judging a person based on what happened to them. For example, if someone goes bankrupt while doing business, we would evaluate the kind of person they are by looking at how they responded to the situation rather than the fact they went bankrupt.

   All kinds of things can happen to people in life. We are living with countless other people, the climate and weather continue to change in unpredictable ways, and the changes brought about by people developing new things are continuously being intertwined with each other. The way of the world is fundamentally something that people cannot control. But when I observe the patients I meet, they are unable to accept this nature of the world. For example, a patient who struggles with anxiety hopes that something will not happen but then suffers when they see signs that it will. "It doesn't matter what happens. Whatever happens, I will do my best." If we maintain this kind of mindset, our anxiety will disappear. It is good to live life without expecting anything since anything can happen.

   The reason why something happens is because there was some inevitable reason for it to occur. And the result is not something that we can change. The only thing we can do is respond appropriately to that result.

   For example, let us imagine that your child overslept on a day they had to take a test. When they wake up, they see that they have completely missed their first test. What should you do when this happens? Should you criticize them saying, "Nice going. Sleeping in on test day…" and rush them to school? Or should you say, "You've failed the test so just give up." If they blame themselves or give up, even if they take the remaining tests, it will be hard for them to do justice to themselves. Should not they at least try to do well on the remaining tests? To do this, it is important to explain calmly to them, "We can't do anything about what already happened. This kind of thing has probably happened before in school, and so you should first go to school and talk to your teacher. And since you had a good night's sleep, you'll be in better shape mentally, so you'll be in a good state to take the rest of your tests. Don't worry and just take the rest of the tests with a calm mind." This is a good way to console your child and help them react in a healthy way. In fact, psychotherapy is also about helping patients have healthy reactions. The important thing is actually reacting in a healthy way and paying close attention to how we are reacting.

2. **Being free from favors and rejection**

   Many of the patients I see are burdened by favors and rejection. As we live our lives, we will both ask and receive favors. However, life will become tiresome if we are not able to deal with favors well. There are people who will not often meet others because they find favors to be burdensome, people who live feeling bad because they turned down favors from others, and people who get angry because they were rejected by others.

But I think words like "favors" or "rejection" are not the right words. This is because these words create burden in those who hear them or use them. And so I believe we need to change the way we think about favors and rejection. I see it as explaining our situation well to others rather than asking for favors, and doing as much as we can while letting others know of my circumstances rather than rejecting them.

If the goal is to explain our situation well to others, then first of all we lessen the burden as the speaker. This is because as long as others have heard us, we have accomplished our goal. Additionally, others need to know our situation to decide whether or not they can help us. When we are close with someone, we can easily talk or listen to them. In fact, some may even say they feel bad we have not told them about a bad situation. Afterwards, it is up to the person who heard our story to do something. It is not something that we as the person telling the story can control.

As for the listener, if they understand it not in terms of rejecting or accepting a favor but rather doing what they can to help, they will always be able to do at least something for the speaker. First of all, simply listening well helps. And if the listener explains that their circumstances are such and which is why they are able to do some things but not others, and then they do what they are able to do, there will be less of a reason to feel bad. Also it is very possible that we who are listening are but one of several people. Since someone who is struggling usually reaches out to many people, we do not necessarily have to be the only ones helping them, as others may even be able help them more.

We cannot do the things we cannot do for someone. Though I may sound like a broken record, such is the principle of the world. And so we must transform our perspective from "favors" or "rejection" to "doing things that we can for each other" and internalize it. Doing this changes the way we accept and carry out things, which makes things less hard on us and allows us to continue to maintain good relationships.

3. **Greeting others well**

Some people think that greeting others first means that they are inferior. However, greeting is an expression that says, "I have no animosity towards you. I want to be friends with you." It is said that greeting people by shaking one's right hand began as a way to confirm that neither person was carrying a weapon in their hand. Whether it is because of this, greeting creates a more relaxed atmosphere. On the other hand, if a person does not greet us, we will constantly worry about them. We will continue to be in a state of anxiety since we do not know what that person will do to us. Even if it is not to that extreme, we will feel awkward due to the uncomfortable atmosphere of the situation. Also, not greeting others can lead to misunderstandings, such as thinking, "Is that person disrespecting me?"

I see greeting others as a way to make the foundation of our lives more pleasant. This is the reason why it is a good idea to hold a housewarming party for your neighbors when you move to a new area. Once, something surprising happened when I went to a restaurant with another psychiatrist. After setting our table with spoons and chopsticks, he then did the same for the people sitting the table next to us. By doing that, though we did not interact with the people next to us, we did not worry at all about them, and if there was something we needed, they helped. It was a pleasant and friendly atmosphere. But this is not always easy. If the person lacks wisdom and is not mentally healthy, they may not even be able to think of doing this. This is because what we are doing here is something that we are able to do without being disappointed in the result on the basis of having a clear understanding that we are beings that all live together. Also the fact that a person able to create such a good atmosphere is proof that they have the ability to observe others well and greet them appropriately. In other words, they are able to clearly see reality as it is and act accordingly.

Once I read a story about a carpenter in some book. The carpenter spent his whole life building houses, and he had a long-term partner who was a businessman. The businessman would draw up a project for commission, and the carpenter would go out and build the house. They worked together like this for a long time. Eventually the carpenter grew old and wanted to retire. He wanted to spend more time with people he was close to and also wanted to do other things. And so he told the businessman that he wanted to retire. The business man then requested that the carpenter build just one more house. The carpenter agreed, but did a terrible job because he did not want to do it. When he finished building the house and handed over the keys to the businessman, the businessman told him, "this house is a present I'm giving you" and gave the keys back to the carpenter. The carpenter ended up doing a terrible job building his own house.

I often tell this story to patients who are caught up in greeting others. Everyone in the world is a home we live in, our furniture, our kitchen. My clinic is on the fourth floor of a seven-story building, and all the people in that building are my homes. If we ignore those people, do not greet them, and do not help them, we are no different than the carpenter who did a terrible job building his own house. Interpersonal relationships are our homes and the air we breathe. Building good relationships by greeting others is a wise and easy gift we can give ourselves. Greeting others is a way to take the lead in our own lives.

4. **Not lying**

One of the five Buddhist precepts is to refrain from lying. Telling the truth is also one of the ten perfections (pāramī) of a bodhisatta.

We have to look closely at the properties of lying. First of all, when we lie, we are giving false information to others. Since they have no choice but to make decisions based on such information, what would happen to them as a result? Secondly, in some cases lying means that we are committing two wrongdoings. For example, if a student tells their mother they are going to after-school academy but goes to see a movie instead, they are committing two wrongdoings, first by skipping the academy to see a movie, and second by lying to their mother.

We lie thinking that it will help us. However, this is not the case. How can our minds be at ease if we have to keep worrying about concealing a lie? Also, we may even have to continue telling other lies to conceal that lie. This is definitely not helpful to our mental health. And what happens when that lie is later discovered? Afterwards, people will not trust us at first. And this will put us in a difficult situation as people will constantly challenge whether or not what we said is true. In the end, this can lead to the person who lied being shunned by others, which makes life difficult inside and out.

On the other hand, if we tell the truth even if we did something wrong, the situation will quickly resolve itself. Let us say that the student who had skipped the academy to go to a movie came home and told the truth. They may get into trouble initially, but the seeds of trust will grow in the minds of their parents, who will think "our child is remarkable. I can trust what they say!" There is a nurse I have incredible trust in. This nurse always tells me when she makes a mistake. I was actually relieved when she told me about a mistake she made since she had been doing well up to the point.

The reason why people lie even though the logic of lying is such is because they lack wisdom. If we look at the "Discourse on Declarations (2)" in the Aṅguttara Nikāya (AN 8.68), we will find a section on the noble words that a Noble One uses. A Noble One says that they have seen and heard what they have actually seen and heard. They do not embellish what they have seen and heard. However, we have a habit to embellish when we talk. There are times when we do this even when we do not have any particular intention to lie. Take a close look at how you are speaking. Also, we often say things like, "I've thought about this and…" without actually having thought about it. We say this liberally since thoughts are not visible and therefore cannot be verified by others. These are not the words of a Noble One.

A Noble One will also say that they know what they know and do not know what they do not know. This is incredibly wise because we will not run into problems if we tell the truth. On the other hand, if we tell lies, we will run into a lot of problems since we have to keep lying so that we do not get caught. This is something we can understand easily if we think of the example of the student who went to go see a movie. Also, when we lie, others can sense something wrong, meaning our mood, actions, expressions, and way of speaking are not natural when we lie. Though we might be able to get away with it at the moment, some form of doubt will remain subtly in the minds of those who heard us lying. Sooner or later, the truth will eventually reveal itself.

I said in the beginning of the lecture that in Buddhism, there are things called mental factors which perform mental functions. If we observe the cognitive process, we will discover that unwholesome mental factors are very bad for us. When we tell lies, unwholesome mental factors will arise in the *javana* stage of the cognitive process, and a countless amount of these *javanas* will arise every second. And at the same time, all of these *javanas* will remain as our karma and lead to bad things. In other words, greed, hatred, and ignorance will arise, creating a foundation for mental illness. For some people, obsessive-compulsive disorder will emerge on this foundation, and for other people, anxiety will emerge.

There is the following saying among Jewish proverbs: "the greatest punishment given to a liar is that other people won't believe them even when they're telling the truth." Someone who is not trusted cannot do anything, and an unpleasant life will await them. This is something we should always remember.

5. **Keeping promises**

   Keeping promises is another one of the ten things that a bodhisatta must cultivate to become a Buddha. It is called "the adhiṭṭhāna pāramī" or the perfection of determination, and it means always doing what we determined to do.

   Promises have a big influence on our interpersonal relationships. How well someone keeps their promises is a direct measure of how well they can be trusted. If we do not keep our promises, it will become easy to be emotionally isolated as we will be excluded by others. One businessman once told me that he considers people without credibility to be corpses. They are people who just come and go in the world without being able to do anything. As people, we need help from others as we are not able to survive on our own, but if we do not have any credibility, who would lend us a hand? As a result, we will not be able to do anything.

   If we keep easily making and breaking promises, we will end up not trusting ourselves. Nowadays, people will often come across a friend they have not seen in a long time and greet them by saying "let's go out to eat sometime," but will then soon forget about it. But if these things continue to build up, even they will affect us negatively. We have all probably experienced a time when we had told a friend we would go out to eat with them sometime but did not stay in touch for a while. Then suddenly it would come up in our minds and we would feel bad about it. If we look at it from a Buddhist perspective, even if we make a promise in passing, it will definitely remain as karma and will at some moment suddenly come to fruition.

   In the past, I also used to easily make and break promises. One day, after seeing how it was negatively affecting my life, I made up my mind to fix this and now I do not do it anymore. The method is simple. All we have to do is make the determination that "I will keep any promise that I make" and carry it out. However, it can be hard to follow such a rule. In particular, if we make promises easily, it will become really hard for us to keep them. However, if we thoroughly assess whether or not we can keep a promise and only make those promises that we can keep, we will definitely be able to keep all of our promises. As this builds up, we will earn the trust of others, and our lives will work out well. Living will become less burdensome.

6. **Conversing well**

   Conversations are also important, as they play a big role in our interpersonal relationships. If we are able to converse well, we will not have issues with our interpersonal relationships, and it will also be possible for us to not have many mental health problems. Conversation is directly linked to mental health, to the point where our ability to converse can be considered as a measure of our mental health.

The basic state of mind one should have when conversing with others is to be considerate. Just as we are the most important thing in the world to us, others are also the most important thing in the world to them. Just as we have a reason for thinking what we think, others will also have a reason for thinking what they think. We are implicitly self-centered, but as long as we maintain seeing us and others on an equal level, we will be able to converse smoothly.

The important thing in conversation is to both speak and listen sufficiently. If we are speaking first, we should sufficiently say what we set out to say. Speaking sufficiently means asking for someone's understanding when they try to cut us off by saying, "Sorry, let me say a little more." Afterwards we should sufficiently listen to what others have to say. Just as we have spoken sufficiently, we should make sure that others are also able to speak their minds sufficiently. If we can continue to do this well, we can have conversations without any big problems.

There are three components to conversation. The person who is speaking, the person who is listening, and the silence when no one is speaking. If we understand these three components well and use them appropriately, we will not have any problems in with conversing.

If there is something that we want to say, or something that others want to hear or will benefit from, we should say it. If we look at people who struggle with conversation, in many cases they think they have to talk even when there is nothing to say. They worry about how others will see them if they do not talk. But while we like people who are good at speaking, we also feel good about people who listen to us well. Therefore, if we have nothing to say, we should just listen. When listening, listen with the mindset that others' experiences are our own, since just as our experience broadens when we read a book or watch a documentary, our experience will also broaden when we listen to others' conversations.

For example, if someone talks about their trip to Hawaii, listen attentively and think about it as an opportunity to learn, "ah, this is what Hawaii is like." Since listening attentively means that we are actively participating in the conversation, others will feel that we are actively engaging with them. So if there is nothing to say, just relax and listen attentively. In some ways, while we have to speak well just to break even, listening can be a profitable business. It is said that psychiatrists are "good listeners," and the doctor who I had mentioned as an example when talking about greeting others well is always a good listener. Therefore, his colleagues would say things like this, "hey, you should contribute too, rather than just listening. Don't just take all of the benefits." We need strength to survive and strength comes from experience. Yet, it is clear that our experiences alone are limited. Therefore, being a good listener is something that benefits us.

There may be times when neither we nor others have anything to say. In such situations where both parties are silent, some people feel anxious. They feel like something is off, like not they are not close with the other person, or that they will not see them again in the future. However, when silence occurs during a conversation, all we have to do is just be comfortable. Enjoy the silence. While people do not really like those who seem anxious, they definitely do not dislike people who seem comfortable. In fact, there is nothing as attractive as being comfortable with someone even if there is nothing going on. Also, people enjoy entertaining and useful conversations, but become tired when a conversation continues pointlessly. Moreover, entertaining and useful conversations do not just happen. There is usually effort involved such as remembering something funny or collecting useful information. Also, there is an innate component to having a sense of humor.

It is also important to find one's place in a conversation. We do not necessarily have to say something useful since someone who knows the topic well can do that, and we do not necessarily have to be funny as we can just have a positive response towards someone who is funny. Just as it is strange to try to be the center of attention at someone else's birthday party, there is no need to try to always be the center of attention. Just as it is our place to simply applaud and enjoy eating at someone else's birthday party, likewise during conversation we should speak, listen, or just enjoy silence depending on the situation.

If we do the things that I have discussed up to this point, we will have no difficulties conversing. However, we tend to make things hard on ourselves. We often get hung up on something and keep trying to force the conversation. After realizing this myself in my 40s, I have continued to practice conversing smoothly. Thanks to that, I am now able to have more comfortable conversations.

There is one more thing to keep in mind when speaking. If we only talk about what is in our minds or our reactions when speaking, we will not have any problems. However, criticizing or attacking others can be problematic. For example, let us say that two people fell in love and got married. However, the husband is extremely busy at work and always comes home late. And so one day the wife says the following, "It's lonely here at home and I'm having a hard time since you're not here. I didn't think our marriage would be like this. I can't help but wonder if this is what marriage is like." To this, most people won't say, "What's wrong with you? Why are you thinking this way?" Rather, it's normal to respond by saying, "Ah it must be hard being alone. I'll try to find a way to come home earlier." On the other hand, if the wife says, "Is this what you married me for, to get me into this situation" and criticizes the husband, the husband will react accordingly. In truth, the husband does not know how the wife is doing while he is at work. But if the wife does not talk about her situation and how she is feeling but rather just criticizes the husband, the husband will also have something to say. The husband may be working hard for the family, or he may have no choice given his current situation. If the husband ends up firing back, it may lead to an argument, and both the husband and wife may feel hurt.

Therefore, when speaking, especially in situations where there may be conflict, we must practice only speaking our minds or our reactions. We need to find a way to let others know what' is going on without provoking them. The nature of conversation is not just speaking and listening, it is also sharing our minds with others. And so, we need be considerate of others. This means thinking about their situation and reacting accordingly. It is like moving an orchid that has become wilted from air conditioning to clean air to give it life.

7. **Living fairly**

One of the things people are most sensitive about is fairness in relationships. The moment we feel like someone is not treating us fairly, we feel repulsion. We think, "That person neglects and disregards me." and will react against it. This is the reason why we experience resistance from others when we speak and act in a self-centered way, even though we may be implicitly self-centered.

For example, let us say we talk about the faults of a friend when they are not with us. It is not fair then to tell our friends who have talked about our faults when we were not there saying, "how could you do this as a friend?" Just as we have done it, it is only fair that others do the same. And so, we should respect others just as we respect ourselves. Fairness between ourselves and others is essential to relationships.

8. **Not cutting off relationships**

We are beings that need help from others while we live our lives. And we ourselves also help others while we live. If we look at the tombstone of steel magnate Andrew Carnegie, we can see that he understood this well and put it into practice. The Tombstone says, "Here lies a man who knew how to enlist in his service better men than himself."

We also meet various people while living. Among them are people who we feel close to, those we feel distant from, and people we do not want to encounter. Some people cut off relationships with people who they feel distant from or do not want to encounter. However, it is better to maintain relationships, as distant or as close as they may be. People who seemed distant can become close, while those close to us can become distant. Such is the nature of human relationships. And because of this, if we cut off relationships based on emotions or judgment, it may be a big loss.

As people, we may change over time. Likewise, others may also change over time. Furthermore, people always have a positive and a negative side to them. There are bad aspects to a good person, and good aspects to a bad person. There are times when someone we trust disappoints us, and other times when someone we did not like is good to us. In this way, people are very complex and variable. It is important to always be aware of this.

This can also be explained through the following analogy. There are times when the food at a restaurant we visit often suddenly changes. Though there may be many reasons for this, it is possible that the change occurred due to some kind of temporary situation. And so if this happens, it is a good idea go back to that restaurant once or twice more so that we can truly know what is going on. Let us say that we did not go back and instead never went to that restaurant again after being disappointed one time. What do you think will happen then? We would just lose a good restaurant. Likewise, it is generally good to have this kind of mindset about people. Otherwise, we will easily be disappointed in people, leading us to cut off more and more relationships until we finally end up alone.

I will give an example. Let us say that there is a student who considers someone in their class to be their enemy. How would this student feel? Going to school will be difficult for them. But could that student be able to get rid of that person, or completely change their minds about hating them? When human relationships are uncomfortable, we need to practice being with that discomfort. This means looking closely at what is making us feel uncomfortable and accepting the uncomfortable feeling as it is. If we try to get rid of it or push back against it, things will get more complicated. One of life's ironies is that we often seal our fate by trying to avoid it. Even if the situation may be difficult or uncomfortable, we have no choice but to carry on. But as we do this, our outlook will start to change. Try to do things while being curious by saying, "let's just see what happens."

9. **Cultivating wisdom**

   I have repeatedly talked about the importance of cultivating wisdom while lecturing on Buddhist psychotherapy. So here I will move on by emphasizing one more time that wisdom arises through observation.

10. **Having an open mind**

    It was during the time when I attended the conference on hypnosis in America in 1995. After the morning sessions ended, I went to the welcome party that took place at the courtyard of the hotel. The hotel staff were preparing the party, when one of them accidentally broke a plate. Everyone was startled. Right then, the person who gave a lecture on self-hypnosis that moment shouted while laughing, "the party has started!" Though in that situation some people may have thought, "what is that staff member thinking. Is he trying to ruin the party" and been irritated because the lecturer was able to handle the situation with an open mind, the party began on a pleasant note.

    At that conference, after the morning sessions and before lunch, there was a time when three or so people came out and told jokes. Since people of all kinds of backgrounds and experiences were gathered together, they set it up in a way to loosen up an atmosphere that can easily become rigid. Because of this people at the conference were able to spend their time laughing and being comfortable.

    Having an open mind means that there is a lot of empty space in our minds. This means that we have the room to pay close attention to others. Let us imagine that our minds are completely filled with something. For example, if our minds are completely filled up, would we be able to let others into our minds? It is therefore very important to have an open mind.

    When we are with others, we need to create space for them. It is especially important to create this kind of space for people that we often spend time with. Although I too struggle with this since I am busy with practicing meditation and giving lectures, we must create space for our family. Only this way, we can be a family that supports each other. Here space means both physical space/time and mental space. While we create physical space and time so that others can enter into it, we must also allow their thoughts and emotions to enter our space. In some ways, I think such openness is necessary for us to be able to truly coexist with others.

It is fun and comfortable to be with a humorous person. And it seems that humor too comes from openness. If we confront each other or create a contentious situation, it can be easy to suddenly get angry. But a person who is open-minded can possess the wisdom to make everyone laugh. Humor is a flower that blossoms from openness.

Something that we really need in life is the ability to adjust. Of course, humor is one way to do this. If we can just turn a difficult situation that we encounter into something that is good for us, living life will not be so difficult. We cannot avoid difficult situations. We will always encounter hardships, and in turn we must overcome them well. I pity the type of person who creates problems in their relationships when things start to get difficult. Such a person will eventually fall apart. This is because when things are good they manage to get along fine, but when they inevitably encounter something that is hard and difficult, they are unable to overcome it.

In some ways, it seems like Buddhism also teaches the ability to adjust. We are unable to move in the face of difficulties that we encounter while we live our lives. What this means is that we cannot avoid suffering. When we experience suffering, the method of turning it into something less painful is what Buddhism calls wisdom, and the ultimate solution to suffering is nirvana.

11. **Having a broad view**

When I think about the patients who seek treatment from me, usually their view is very narrow. They are only interested in themselves or their families. And they nitpick a lot over their gains and losses. They also really emphasize things like efficiency. At first, I did not know that these were characteristics of poor mental health, but later on I realized that these were all part of the main problem. After I discovered this, I began focusing my treatment on these things. As a result, I was able to see that when my patients broadened their view, they were able to recover their mental health and live well.

Having a narrow view leads to poor mental health while having a broad view leads to good mental health. It is not just the things that we do or the people close to us that affect us, but rather all the things that happen in the world affect us. People who have a broad view see this truth as it is, but people who have a narrow view think that these things are irrelevant to them. And so having a broad view means that we have the wisdom to see things in the right way.

People with a narrow view try to avoid meeting people they do not want to meet or people who seem like they do not matter to them. But they cannot always avoid meeting such people. And so, they find it very difficult when such meetings occur. However, if we look at the reality of the situation, even someone telling us about things such as their travels can be helpful to us. Meeting others is beneficial. People with a narrow view do not understand this and so they do not want to listen to others because they think that it is irrelevant to them. On the other hand, people with a broad view understand that everything is relevant to them and so they see everything as interesting and have no trouble meeting anyone. They are able to get along well with others. However, this does not mean that they are sacrificing themselves and living solely for others. They see themselves and others in a balanced way and act with the mindset that others are like themselves.

And so people with a narrow view are always troubled by this and that, while people with a broad view live without being troubled by anything. For example, let us say that there is a doctor who does not want to see patients. Such a doctor does not see patients but rather just looks at the monitor. How hard must it be for them to do something they do not want to do. However, is it even possible for a doctor to not see patients? One day, the doctor too ends up becoming a patient. And when he becomes a patient, he too wants to meet a good doctor. This is actually how everything is in the world.

I think it will help to tell a story about the Dalai Lama with regard to this. When we look at the Dalai Lama giving talks, sometimes people give him something to drink. When they do, the Dalai Lama momentarily stops speaking to thank the person, and then continues. Even though he could take this for granted, he always thanks the person. He is being respectful to each and every person as much as possible.

Once the Dalai Lama told the following story. At a Dhamma talk in Dharamshala, India in 2009 he said that whenever he would say something, people would be extremely inspired, but he did not know why. And then when he went to America, he said that he saw some homeless person smoking and drinking and told him, "I think you should stop doing one or the other." Then, that person began sobbing uncontrollably. I think that was natural for that beggar to have such a reaction. After all, some monk whose name he did not know just approached him and encouraged him by saying something helpful with genuine concern for his well-being. Who in this person's normal life would have done such a thing? Everyone would have just tried to avoid him. The beggar was inevitably brought to tears because he felt the Dalai Lama's genuine concern. And it is because the Dalai Lama always treats others in this genuine way that they are moved by the things he says.

Speaking about society for a moment, these days there are many multicultural families. Yet these people must be well established for society to be safe. If these people are discriminated against in society such as at school or at work, they will develop antagonistic feelings towards society. And what would happen if these people act on such antagonistic feelings? All kinds of bad things including violent acts would occur.

Seeking what we want while not creating enemies is a way to truly take care of ourselves. If we try to accomplish things even if it means creating enemies, then we will receive what is appropriate in return. We need to be able to clearly see this truth that all people and all things are connected to us. Though we must do well for ourselves, it is only truly good when the society we live in is also safe and well. This is not a truth that just applies to a specific country, but one that applies to the entire world.

The best Buddhist practice for broadening one's view is cultivating the Four Immeasurables. It is cultivating the four minds of the loving kindness of loving all beings, the compassion of wishing that all beings be free from suffering, the sympathetic joy of genuinely enjoying the happiness of others, and based on those three, the equanimity of calmly seeing people as they are. As I have said earlier, I feel the most at ease and the most unhindered when these Four Immeasurables are established. I feel like I can be thankful even if someone hits me. If we cultivate the Four Immeasurables, we can live with a broad mind and a big heart.

12. **Developing the Ability to Empathize**

I have talked before about developing the ability to empathize. I recommend that you look at "Practicing Empathy" (p. 79–80) for details. Here, I will talk about three kinds of people who especially need the ability to empathize.

The first kind of person who really needs to have the ability to empathize are parents. This is because just as much as the child sees their parents as special, the influence that parents have on their child is extremely powerful. We need to always remember that even a small mistake of a parent who is not able to empathize with their child will eventually come back in a significant way. The second kind of person are teachers. Though these days there is a tendency for teaching to become professionalized, even so teachers can have a tremendous influence on their students. This is because students still see their teachers as special. It is commonly said that even if a child is raised poorly by their parents, if a teacher is able to fix them up well, they can grow into a good person. Even if they learned some bad things from their parents, if they meet a good teacher at school, they can develop good character. An example where both parents and teachers failed is the case of Shin Changwon, who was infamous for escaping from prison. It is said that he once said the following, "I was abused by my parents, and when I went to school, the teachers did the same to me. I can't trust anyone." The third kind of person who needs to have the ability to empathize are those in religious organizations. People consider those such as monks, ministers, and priests to be special. They see them as a guiding light that will help them live a good life. To that extent, these religious figures can have a powerful influence on those who follow them.

According to Freud, we are composed of the id, the ego, and the superego. The three kinds of people that I have discussed up to this point can help us develop a healthy superego. Therefore it is important to make an effort to know the minds of others as they are and treat them accordingly.

13. **Thinking less and being true to reality**

I have also talked a lot about this up to this point. If the mind goes to the past or the future, we become mentally unhealthy, whereas if the mind is in the present, we become mentally healthy. For tips on staying in the present, I will just remind everyone that there are ways to do this such as doing things without making noise and telling ourselves when the mind has gone to the past that "the past has gone," and when the mind has gone to the future that "the future hasn't come yet so we don't know" and then returning to the present.

14. **Doing things that benefit us**

When I think about the people I meet in my clinic, I notice that they do things that are not beneficial to them. For example, this happens for people who have big egos, which causes them problems. I think that having a big ego is a serious illness. These days there are a lot of discussions on self-esteem. However, self-esteem is different from ego. Self-esteem means cherishing yourself, whereas ego is saying "This is who I am. Don't touch this." People with self-esteem will do anything that helps them, while people with a big ego will be stubborn about things and may not do what is beneficial to them. Sometimes they may even do things that are harmful to them. They also do not like it when others try to help them because they think they are doing it out of pity.

People who have big egos will think like this, "How can I, a college graduate, do something like this!" without any regard to reality, even if that is the only thing that they are actually able to do. In reality, we have to do the things that we are able to do right now. If we do not do anything we will be stuck in place. On the other hand, as we do things that we are able to do, we will increase our skills. And as our skills increase, we can accordingly head in the direction of doing things that we want to do. And so, I recommend to my patients to do things that they are able to do. I tell them to go out and earn money if they can and to clean their home if they can. Whatever it may be, we need to do the things that we are able to do. If we can see things in this way and also live our lives like this, we will keep growing every day. And our mental problems will disappear too.

Therefore, when I meet a patient who has problems with their ego, I start by treating it first. This is because ego is not helpful to our lives. To help a patient see the same thing in a different way, I go through the process of observing them carefully and understanding them, after which exert the appropriate amount of effort to treat them so that they naturally shift their point of view on their own.

Rather than being bound be something like ego, we need to look closely at the things that help us and do those things. Doing things based on greed, hatred, and ignorance do not help us. If we look at something we are doing and find that it is not helping us or others, we should stop doing it. All we have to do is see it as follow: we should do things that are good for us and others. And if a harmful thought that is connected with greed, hatred, and ignorance arises while we are carefully observing our mind moment to moment, we should immediately stop it. This is how we can become mentally healthy. If we do a lot of training to focus on the present moment, we can immediately observe all the thoughts that arise subtly moment to moment. Once we get to this point, we can immediately stop a harmful thought as it arises. We then will not fall into situations where we are mentally unhealthy.

If we experience psychosis, with the exception of a few special circumstances, we must take medication. Because psychosis means that there has been a great disturbance in the brain's neurotransmitters, we must use medicine to quickly correct the situation. If we are not careful, our physical health may suffer as we will not be able to sleep, and we may do other harmful things such as fighting or harming others. However, to successfully stop taking medicine and to prevent relapse, we ultimately need to be able to cut off harmful thoughts. If we are not able to deal with harmful thoughts by observing the mind, there is no guarantee that we can be free from taking medication or that we will not enter relapse.

Even people who are not suffering from psychosis or who are not mentally unhealthy need to practice controlling their minds regularly. No one knows when they will encounter suffering. Even if we are living comfortably now, we are immediately affected if something bad happens. We are also unable to escape from the influence of things that are inputted into us moment to moment. Therefore, whether it is our emotions, thoughts, intentions, perceptions, or desire, we need to have the ability to carefully observe all the things that are inputted into us, keep the things that help us, and stop the things that do not help us.

15. **Reading books**

Power comes from experience. However, there is a limit to the amount of experiences we can have. We are limited by time since we will live for at most around a 100 years, limited by the area that we live in, and limited by the things that we do. There are also other factors that limit our experiences aside from this.

One way to escape from such limitations is to read books. Though it is in an indirect way, we can meet various people, see into all corners of the world, and obtain all kinds of information through reading. We can then take the things we have learned and apply them to our lives to make things better. These days, there are various mediums aside from books through which we can expand our experiences. However, it seems like the most effective way is still to read books.

There are people however who read books in the wrong way. Some people read only to confirm what they already know. This is something we should not do. Books are written by people who have had some kind of experience and felt that there was some value to sharing it. Therefore, we need to stop our own thoughts when reading books. It is good to read with the following mindset, "I will share the experience with the author. I will try entering the world that the author leads me into." In this way, we can overcome our own limitations little by little.

To do this, we have to choose the right books. This is because while there is obviously a need to filter out books that are not good, we will benefit a lot more from reading good books rather than books that are just mediocre. Back in 1990, I once organized a book club for 10 years. When I look back at that time, I remember that whenever we had read one good book, it seemed like there were tens of books we could read related to it. Books recommended by experts are often good. And it is also important to read books that are categorized as classics. Classics are books that remain relevant among the countless books that appear and fade away over time. Because classics are books that people share with each other and preserve for the future, it is important to read them in-depth. If we carefully select and read good books like this, we will develop the ability to see the world correctly and respond to it well. We will also improve our ability to choose and read good books.

Reading books is also important for children. Children who read books can unlock a hidden potential. No matter how much potential we have, if we do not meet the conditions for them to manifest, they will never be expressed. However, as we engage in a broad range of experiences including reading books, we may meet the conditions for those hidden things to reveal themselves.

16. **Delaying gratification**

I take a rather late summer vacation. Usually, I go around mid-August. Even though it is hard from late July to early August because of the heat, it becomes easier to bear when I think about being able to rest in just a few more days.

The American psychiatrist and author of the book *The Road Less Traveled*, M. Scott Peck once treated a worker who kept procrastinating. When Peck first met her, he thought that the person felt resentment towards her superiors and began treating her on that. However, it was not effective at all. Then one day Peck happened to ask the following, "When you eat cake, which part do you eat first?" The patient responded, "I eat the most delicious part first." From this Peck realized, "the problem with this person is that she does the things she likes first," and recommended that she put off doing the things she liked. Once he began that kind of treatment, the patient no longer put off her work.

If we do the things we like first, we will not want to do what comes afterwards. On the other hand, if we put off doing the things we like until later and do the things we do not like first, even the things that we do not really like become tolerable. This is because we also get hope as the things we like await us. This is also wisdom in life.

17. **Living within our means**

We will not struggle at all as long as we live within our means. However, whether it is regarding money or knowledge or relationships, if we do not do things within our means, we will struggle. For example, how hard would it be for someone if they had been negligent about their relationships and suddenly expected to have a lot of guests to their wedding? Also, how hard would it be on someone to pretend they know something they do not, or for someone to pretend they have a lot of money when they do not. Even though this is the truth of the matter, there are many people who do not live within their means. Additionally, many people will complain about their present situation. However, there is a necessary process that inevitably led to our present situation. This is the only way it works according to the law of cause and effect. Knowing this and having an attitude of accepting our present circumstances is necessary for mental health.

Among mental illnesses, depression can be explained in this context. A lot of things are discussed as being the cause for depression, but in my opinion, depression can come to the extent that the way we are actually living differs from the way we want to live. What this means is that we lose the will to live because we want to live in a certain way, but we are not able to. Because we cannot accept our present situation, we will do various harmful things to ourselves such as blaming others and blaming ourselves, which will make the situation even worse. People with depression usually have a hard time getting things started in the morning. They struggle because the moment they open their eyes they have to live a life that they do not want to live. Though this can also be explained from a biochemical perspective, the physical does not come first. The mind comes first.

We need to make sure that the only thing in our minds is our current life. We can only have one life. We can never have two lives. And there are reasons why our current life is the way it is. Therefore, if our current life is difficult, we need to find out why and change it for the better. We need to cherish this one life that we are living right now and keep working on it. If we do not do this and just wish for things that are not there, our current lives will never improve.

References

1. Bodhi B (trans) (1995). The middle length discourses of the Buddha: a translation of the Majjhima Nikāya. Simon and Schuster, New York, p 887
2. Bodhi B (trans) (2012). The numerical discourses of the Buddha: a translation of the Aṅguttara Nikāya. Wisdom Publications, Boston, MA, pp 232–233
3. Bodhi B (trans) (2017). The Suttanipata: an ancient collection of the Buddha's discourses together with its commentaries (the teachings of the Buddha). Wisdom Publications, Boston, MA, p 296

Chapter 5
Understanding People with Mental Illnesses

The effectiveness of treatment depends on the therapist's ability to understand people. If the therapist understands the patient well and prescribes treatment that suits them, the results of the treatment will be positive. If not, it will inevitably be negative. A therapist must therefore develop the ability to understand people.

How Do We Establish Relationships?

A therapist is someone meets with people who are suffering from mental illnesses. What kind of mindset, what kind of attitude should the therapist have? Additionally, what should they do when they meet the patient and how should they do it? In this chapter, we will look at these questions.

The most basic component to treatment is developing a relationship with the patient. If this isn't established, the therapist can't go onto the next stage. Once the relationship between the therapist and the patient becomes firmly established, the therapist is then able to move forward towards understanding. That understanding is the treatment.

One of the things a therapist must pay attention to in their relationship with patients is "mannerisms." It is the attitude of seeing the patient more or less as "someone who we see often" when interacting with them. But does the patient think the same way? First of all, the patient has trouble even coming to the clinic. They go back and forth between the hope that they will get better and the thought of giving up thinking, "might as well just live like this." And so they wander around endlessly like this until they finally knock on the door of the clinic. Sidney Tarachow's book, *An Introduction to Psychotherapy*, says that a patient will never seek out treatment unless they are in an urgent situation. They only come to the clinic when they realize that something terrible might happen if they keep going this way. It is a very desperate state of mind. A therapist must not be careless when treating a patient who has

H. Jeon, *Buddhist Psychotherapy*, https://doi.org/10.1007/978-3-030-63098-0_5

come in these circumstances. They must be in tune with the desperate mind of the patient and come face to face with it.

A therapist may believe they are the only one who can diagnose and treat a patient, but this is not the case. A patient will look into the therapist and make subtle diagnoses with their entire body as to whether or not the therapist is skilled, trustworthy, or just doing it as a means to earn money. A therapist must pass this strict test that the patient gives them. If they do not pass the test, the patient will not come to them again. If they do not come, there can be no treatment.

After passing the patient's test, a therapist must remain true to their task. A therapist must not forget that they are there to treat the patient. They must not use patients as just a means to earn money or gain fame. For example, let us say there is a psychotherapist who keeps asking about the stock market while treating a professional stock broker. This is to be expected if it were to help treat the patient, but if not, the therapist should not do this. Just as a surgeon washes their hands before performing surgery, a psychotherapist must have the intent to solely understand and help the patient they are meeting. From the moment they see a patient, they must focus their entire body and mind to treating the patient. They must also do this in a relaxed way, making sure not to give off the impression that they are too focused, as it can become burdensome for the patient.

The patient must be able to look at a therapist and get the impression that "this person is focused on me!" And so a therapist must also sleep well because if they are not well-rested, they may be unfocused when they meet patients. Even if the therapist has other things on their mind, for as long as they are meeting the patient, they need to set those things aside and focus on the patient. While focusing on the patient, the therapist must be able to notice when a patient is unsatisfied and know how to resolve it. A therapist must have this kind of training.

Once all of this is in place and the patient thinks, "this therapist is trustworthy. They only want to treat me. They care more about me than I care about myself" the therapist–patient relationship becomes established. Only when such a foundation is set up can a therapist and a patient become "allies in treatment," which allows the treatment to move forward. Just as an ally in war means that you are fighting on the same side as someone else, an "alliance in treatment" refers to when the therapist allies with the healthy side of a patient and works to transform the unhealthy side of the patient.

If a treatment-oriented relationship is not established between a therapist and a patient, they cannot move onto the next stage. Therefore, a therapist must first focus all their efforts in establishing that therapist–patient relationship. If you think of it like a dance, this relationship is like when the two dance partners are completely synchronized in their movements. A therapist must always establish this relationship regardless of how many times they have seen the patient. Continuing to do such delicate work this way whenever seeing a patient is what the work of treatment is about.

Relaxed Intervention

Once the therapist–patient relationship is established, the therapist must then spend time understanding the patient. They must get a grasp on the patient by listening to them and observing their expressions and actions. Like Sherlock Holmes, a therapist must become someone who is able to see through a patient. However, they cannot be too sensitive as they will become exhausted.

The patient and the therapist have lived different lives. And so what is in their minds is different, how they think is different, and how they speak is also different. What this means is that when the patient says something, a therapist must resist interpreting it in their own language. It is best if a therapist can see inside the mind of the patient. They must be able to stop themselves, enter into the patient, and move together with the patient through their lives. A therapist that moves together with the patient can even see things that occur within the patient that are not visible to them. When this happens, if the therapist reacts by posing a question to the patient, the patient can then realize themselves "ah, there was something going on here!"

To do this, a therapist must get the patient to focus on them. As in hypnosis therapy, the patient can proceed with the treatment while exercising influence on the patient when they are in a focused stated. To this end, the therapist must make it so that the patient is comfortable at all times. They must ensure that the patient is comfortable in the time they are together and feels secure thinking, "even though I'm having a hard time elsewhere, I am comfortable when I'm here!" The patient must be in this comfortable place to be able to speak freely, as they must be the one who speaks first. The general principle is for the therapist to let the patient speak first, and then to speak afterwards when the patient no longer has anything to say. Sometimes, a patient may be late to their appointment making it so that there is not enough time for counseling, but even when this happens the therapist must make sure the patient feels like they have plenty of time. When the therapist is relaxed, they can help the patient not feel pressed for time.

There are also times when the patient's conversation may go completely off topic. When this happens, it is necessary to pivot the topic of the conversation by asking questions or by intervening naturally. Rather than forcing the patient to go a certain direction, the therapist should react appropriately and guide the patient naturally by going into their minds, empathizing with them, and understanding them. The therapist asks questions not because they do not know the answer, but to provide an opportunity for the patient to say something important. This is called an interpretative question. To make an analogy, the therapist's question is like a person in a dark room with a flashlight. Their questions shine the flashlight, guiding the patient towards the light switch so they can turn it on. The right questions help the patient see things.

Special Relationships Built on Top of Normal Relationships

Though the therapist–patient relationship is special, it is always built on top of a normal relationship with kindness and respect at its basis. However, a therapist should not be mindless and treat a patient who is being serious in a friendly way like a waiter at a restaurant greeting customers. An appropriate level of kindness and respect are necessary for a person who is suffering. For example, I usually speak casually with patients who are under 25 years old. However, I do not immediately do this as soon as I meet them. Rather, I begin by speaking formally and speak casually as time goes on. I do this because it is typical for a person in their 60s to speak casually to someone in their 20s once they get to know each other. And so usually a patient in their 20s feels more comfortable when someone like me in my 60s speaks casually to them. Once, I even had someone in their late 30s ask me to speak casually, so I obliged. What important is that I do not speak casually out of my own convenience, but rather do so knowing that it will make the patient feel comfortable while still feeling respected.

Also, as I have said before earlier, when a therapist meets a patient, they must approach the meeting as if it is the last, that there is no tomorrow. This does not mean they should be impatient, but rather than they need to meet patients with the mindset of doing the very best they can in the time they have. The therapist needs to make sure that the meeting does not feel inert. They should always maintain a reasonable level of alertness regardless of how many times they have met the patient and provide them a sense of novelty. This means making sure that the patient has the experience of feeling and knowing something new they meet the therapist every time until the treatment ends.

If we do this, we will come to better understand the patient each time we meet them face to face. If understanding through empathy and the positive cycle of making each meeting new continue, we will build up a clear understanding that has the power of healing. It is extremely important to have a clear understanding in a therapeutic relationship. Understanding itself is treatment. In some ways, a patient develops problems because they are misunderstood. Therefore, having the experience where a patient feels, "Ah, someone does understand me!" is important for their treatment.

Psychotherapy is also sometimes called psychological surgery. This is because the therapist constantly observes the patient's positive side and their negative side on the basis of clear understanding, and they help bring the positive side to life while working on the negative side. When a therapist meets the patient again, they must compare that meeting with the previous meeting and look carefully at what kinds of change occurred in the patient. And if there is a change, they need to react to it. If a positive change occurred, the therapist should keep encouraging the patient. There are times when the patient have gone through a positive change, but people around them such as their family and friends are not able to see it or even say that things have gotten worse. However, even a small change is important progress. If the therapist can recognize this change and react appropriately by sharing in joy with the patient, that itself has an incredible effect on the patient's treatment. Therefore, a therapist must be able to be sensitive to these kinds of things.

Through these kinds of experiences, a patient will come to understand that there are "healthy relationships," and will head in the direction of trying to maintain such relationships in their lives. Freud said that psychotherapy is raising the patient again like a parent raising their child. This means that a therapist must provide the experience of a healthy relationship to the patient so that they can develop new methods for approaching their problems. This is how the "corrective emotional experience" discussed in psychoanalysis can occur.

A concept discussed by psychoanalyst Franz Alexander, corrective emotional experience refers to the following: in the past, someone had a negative experience in a situation that affected their lives negatively. However, through their relationship with the therapist or some other meaningful person, they are now able to have a new healthy experience towards the same situation, which leads to a big change in their lives. This concept is very important in psychotherapy. The character Jean Valjean in the novel *Les Misérables* had this very experience. After spending a long time in prison for stealing a piece of bread, Jean Valjean is released and ends up spending the night at a church. He tries to steal some valuables in the church but is immediately caught by the police. However, the bishop of the church shields Valjean by asking why he did not also take the silver candle holders, which he gives to him. Through this experience, Jean Valjean is able to let go of his hostility towards the world. For the treatment to be successful, a patient must be able to have this kind of experience in the context of psychotherapy.

The Therapist's State of Mind During the First Session

Now, I will point out a few more things in more detail concerning the process of treatment. Though I will somewhat repeat some of the things that I have said before, new things will emerge in this process of repetition. Let us begin by looking at the "first session."

As I have said before already, it is not easy for the patient to even come to the clinic. The therapist must keep in mind that the patient knocked on the doors of the clinic in desperation after wandering endlessly and finally deciding that they have no other choice. There may also be differences in the result of the treatment depending on whether the therapist knows the process that led to the patient coming to the clinic. Therefore, the therapist must learn the details of how the patient came to the clinic. Obviously, a therapist must learn why the patient is suffering and how they have been during that time, but they must also not leave out any details, as minor as they may seem, including things like whether the patient was referred by someone, whether they came after reading a book or a news article, or whether they came after seeing a signboard. Any information about the patient is valuable. That person is contained inside all those things. The more the therapist can know about the patient, the better they can help them.

Here, we will take a moment to revisit the basic position of Buddhist psychotherapy before moving on. Buddhist psychotherapy is based completely on understanding the truth. Therefore, Buddhist psychotherapy sees theories that have not been confirmed as problematic, such as sticking to frameworks like "if someone has a bad relationship with their parents in infancy, they will develop problems." In Buddhist psychotherapy, there is an effort to clearly see as it is the things that arise and what is induced from them, rather than approaching them with thoughts or theories. We must not think that we know something just because we have read in a book. We must be able to clearly distinguish what we know and what we do not know. The work of therapy must proceed on such a foundation.

Now returning to our original discussion, if a therapist has figured out what is going on with the patient, they must then help the patient see themselves clearly. They must help the patient know things such as what kind of state they are in right now and how the people around them are doing as they are. If the patient's family is having a hard time because of them, the therapist must be able to clearly see what needs to be done in order for the patient to get better and be able to propose those things to them without reading into the patient or their family and without taking anyone's side. Only things that are accurate are effective.

Furthermore, the therapist needs to focus on the people rather than the problems. The therapist and the patient are both people. This means that the work of treatment occurs within the meeting of two people and the back and forth conversation that naturally occurs between them. As I have said earlier, the therapist–patient relationship is "a special relationship that is built on top of a normal relationship." The basis of the relationship is the conversation that goes back and forth naturally and the trust that is built between the therapist and the patient. That way a patient will be able to speak their minds freely which will allow the therapist to be able to understand the patient. Anyone who meets someone who understands them feels at ease. They will also feel that they are not alone. This is the feeling that helps the patient evoke the will to follow the path that the therapist sets out for them. It is the result of the therapist going inside the mind of the patient and trying to help the patient be in a better place than they can be on their own. To give an example, one patient who sought me out told me that he does not end up doing the things that other people say he should do, but he does the things that I suggest him to do.

The First Thing that Should Be Done During the First Session

The therapist must do two things in the first session. If the conditions are not right, then they may only be able to do one of them, but it is better to keep a good track of time and do both things if possible.

The first is revealing the characteristics of the problem and the process by which it arose. The therapist should know in detail when the problem started and what kind of process the patient went through to get to the clinic. The therapist must figure out the things that will show them who the patient is, such as what happened to them, how it came to happen, whether they talked about it with others, what they have done to try to solve the problem, or what their usual relationships are like.

Meanwhile, the therapist must carefully examine what is going on in the patient externally and internally. This means clearly distinguishing and figuring out what happened to the patient and how the patient reacted internally to what happened. In particular, the therapist must determine how the patient coped with what happened to them, what kinds of thoughts they had, and what kinds of things arose in their body and mind as they brought up thoughts about the past and future related to what happened.

The most important thing is for the therapist to see clearly. By seeing clearly, they will come to completely understand why the patient became ill. And with that understanding, they need to figure out what measures to take at what time so that some kind of change can occur in the patient and the treatment can start having effects on them. At the same time, the therapist must help the patient have some sort of realization while they are in the process of talking. It is good if the patient comes to think, "this therapist knows my problem well. Though it's not completely clear, my problem came about because of such and such reason. If I spend time with this therapist, I can change!" This way, the patient can actively approach the process of treatment on the basis of trust towards the therapist.

The Second Thing that Should Be Done During the First Session

After doing the first thing that should be done in the first session, namely revealing the present problems of the patient, the second thing that must be done is to understand how the patient had been living up to now. This is because we need to understand who the patient is as well as understanding the problem the patient is facing for the appropriate treatment to take place.

Of course, the therapist continues to deal with the patient's life even after the first session. But the reason why I especially emphasize understanding the way a patient has lived during the first session is so that the therapist does not go all over the place in confusion. If the therapist comes to know the reason why the patient's current problem has inevitably arisen by determining, "this patient spent their childhood in such and such family, and afterwards lived in such and such a way which led to this problem!" they have painted a rough picture of the patient. This means that they have a general grasp on the patient, even though they may need to complete the smaller details of this picture in future sessions. However, the therapist must also not be tied down by this rough picture. They should use it as a general roadmap for what is to come in the future, and should avoid using it to brand a patient as being a certain kind of person.

To understand what the patient went through in their life, the therapist usually begins by asking about their earliest memory. They ask, "what is the earliest memory in your life?" The reason why they ask this is because in many cases there are important things contained in that earliest memory though of course this is not always the case. Also, everyone has an earliest memory. This is because the earliest memory is that of the earliest event in one's life. Without going far back, if someone does not remember what happened before yesterday, then yesterday becomes their earliest memory. The earliest memory may be something that actually occurred and it may not. This is because rather than remembering something that actually occurred as it is, our memory is affected by things such as our brain's state.

For their earliest memory, people usually bring up something that happened when they were around 6 years old. While there are some who remember things that happened before then, including some who have memories of when they were in the womb, this is not common. After asking about the earliest memory, a therapist always asks about how the person felt during their first memory. If they say they do not really know, a therapist can ask how that experience would be if it were happening right now. In this way, the therapist starts with the earliest memory, then the second, then the third, all the way up to when the patient began elementary school. These memories are important. And they also ask casually about the patient's family to figure out what kind of child they were. During this process, the therapist may be able to see a correlation between the relationship the patient had with their family or those close to them at that time and their current problems.

Next, the therapist asks the patient detailed questions such as what it was like when they went to elementary school, how they studied, whether they had good relationships with their friends, if they had any talents, what they wanted to be when they grew up, and whether they had any complexes or difficulties. Here, the therapist should avoid asking questions in a prying manner. After the therapist finishes asking questions about the patient's elementary school life, they then ask about middle school, high school, college, military service, jobs, their love lives or marriage, everything up to the point where they are experiencing their current problem. Meanwhile they always check in to see what the patient did when they faced a difficult situation. Mental problems arise because we have the wrong reactions towards the things that arise in our lives. Therefore, it is extremely important to know how the patient usually deals with these difficult situations.

Dreams

When I see patients, I also ask a lot about their dreams. This is because during the 4 years and 2 months when I received psychoanalysis, I did much of it with dreams, and it was then that I became convinced that dreams are a 100% accurate. I am not the only one. Others who do psychoanalysis or in-depth psychotherapy all work with dreams.

Among dreams, those dreams that are meaningful repeat themselves. This is because a problem that is not resolved repeats itself and appears as a dream. This also means that if that problem is resolved, we will then no longer have dreams associated with it. One of the patients I met repeatedly had dreams about taking the entrance exam to Seoul National University. This is because he was bitter from not getting into the university. As that bitterness was resolved through the process of treatment, the person stopped having those dreams. Also, when a person changes, they first change in their dreams. If a person who struggles with presenting in front of other people dreams of giving a good presentation, they will then actually be able to present well. People who practice Buddhist meditation tend to struggle keeping the precepts, but if they keep the precepts while they are dreaming, they will also do so in real life.

There are other reasons why a therapist asks about a patient's dreams. This is because there are times when a patient dreams in anticipation about the therapist or the treatment prior to meeting the therapist. If the patient recalls something positive about the therapist within their dream, then we can say that the treatment will go smoothly. However, if there's something negative instead, the therapist needs to take the appropriate measures to improve the situation and lead the patient in a direction that will help them better.

Additionally, a therapist can use dreams to help the patient understand themselves. Because we are in a certain state of existence in our dreams, dreams can be used as tools to look into ourselves. In dreams, associations are important. Associations here mean all the thoughts that arise along with a dream. For example, if you dreamed about being chased by a stranger, thinking about a certain friend afterwards is an association. Also, things that come up suddenly while talking about dreams during a session are also associations. If a therapist who heard a patient talk about a dream where a therapist appeared asks the patient if anything comes to mind when they say "therapist," the thing that comes to mind is also an association.

If we follow associations, we can figure out the meaning of the dream. As we follow along the trail of associations, we will naturally come to know, "Ah, this is the reason I had this dream!" This happens even if we take some quiet time after we dream to just calmly write down the associations of that dream. For example, let us say that we met someone and had the impression that they were a good person, but they appeared in our dreams as a con artist. If we follow the associations of that dream when this happens, we will come to find that there was something somewhat suspicious about that person while we were meeting them, as this is something that was amplified, leading to the appearance of a "con artist" in our dream.

Analyzing Past Treatments

There are many cases where a patient has received treatment or therapy in the past. The therapist must look into such treatment. This is very important, because it is possible to repeat past failures during treatment. Therapists have a tendency to think that their treatment will be successful, regardless of how treatments went in the past. However, there is a very high chance, in my opinion more than 90%, that they repeat what happened in the past. If treating a patient was difficult in one circumstance, the therapist is not exempt from this. Therefore, if a patient has received treatment or therapy in the past, the therapist must listen closely to specifically what kind of treatment they underwent, what got better as a result, and what was unsatisfactory about it. And with that as the basis, they need to enter treatment in a different way from the past. If they do it like it was done in the past, the result will be the same.

And if we look at research on the effects of treatment, there are many cases where the results of treatment depend more on the patient rather than the therapist. Treatment works well for a good patient and does not work well for a bad patient. A good patient is one who is motivated to change themselves, has the ability to reflect on themselves, and has worked hard in the past. They are patients who do what they are supposed to do well during treatment. They are patients who maintain a good therapist–patient relationship. A bad patient is one who expects the therapist to solve all their problems, does not put in much effort, does not reflect on themselves much, and has not worked hard in the past. It is hard for someone to have effective results in their treatment if they do not have a firm therapist–patient relationship and are easily swayed.

Something creates suffering in a patient, and that suffering becomes a mental illness. The key to treatment is the method of dealing with that suffering. It works when it deals with suffering in a way that does not cause mental problems. Therefore, a therapist must help the patient understand how they can deal with suffering so that mental problems do not arise and must also help them to be able to change themselves. If the patient reacts in a way that is not in accordance with reality but is rather in conflict with it, the therapist should give the patient a method that is not in conflict with reality and help the patient naturally carry it out. The role of a therapist during treatment is to help the patient realize that they themselves play an important role and to help them slowly change themselves.

Pharmaceutical Therapy and Other Considerations

A therapist must find out how a patient views medication because there are times when medication is necessary. There are a lot of people who are misinformed about mental health medication. The therapist must accurately explain medicine to such people, such as those who believe it destroys brain cells. They must also provide consultation on how to use medicine well.

A patient's economic circumstance is also extremely important. Since patients who do not have much money can only come to the clinic once or twice, the therapist must make it so that those patients are able to do things that help themselves without necessarily having to come to the clinic. Those whose are more well off financially can come to the clinic for a long time and likely have different expectations, so it is good to adjust accordingly.

As I have stressed several times, the effectiveness of treatment depends on the ability of a therapist to understand people. If they are able to understand the patient well and prescribe the treatment that is suitable for them, the results will be positive, whereas it will inevitably be negative in the opposite case. Therefore, a therapist must develop the ability to understand people, and in order to do this, they need to observe people frequently on a day-to-day basis. This is also something that I have said several times up to this point. Though it is important to read books and listen to lectures, we need to train ourselves to look closely at what kind of mindset someone we are dealing with has and how they view the world. We need to look carefully at the principles that drive people and the world. If someone is happy, then we need to look at why they are happy, if they are miserable then why they are miserable, if they have succeeded then how they have succeeded, if they have failed then how they have failed, if they do business well then how they do business well, if they do not do business well then how they do not do business well. If we accumulate such observations over a long time, then we will be able to accurately and quickly understand someone we have met for the first time.

Chapter 6
Methods of Buddhist Psychotherapy

From the perspective of Buddhist psychotherapy, treatment is successful when a patient naturally acquires the three principles of Buddhist psychotherapy and lives according to them. In other words, if the patient clearly understands the properties of the body and mind, knows the principles of the way the world works, and sees the things that happen to them as they are moment to moment and reacts to those things with wisdom to benefit themselves, mental problems will not arise again.

Psychotherapy

Psychotherapy is a method of treating a patient's problems in-depth conversations. It is the process where the therapist and client engage in a therapeutic dialog so that they both understand well the process which led the client to their present psychological problem, and then work together to solve that problem. As a result, psychotherapy is successful if the client is able to realize, "I've lived in such and such way and developed this problem because I didn't resolve such and such issues well. I see that if I do such and such thing to solve this and should look after myself moment to moment!" puts it into practice and improves their mental health.

From the perspective of Buddhist psychotherapy, treatment is successful when a patient naturally acquires the three principles of Buddhist psychotherapy and lives according to them. In other words, if the patient clearly understands the properties of the body and mind, knows the principles of the way the world works, and sees the things that happen to them as they are moment to moment and reacts to those things with wisdom to benefit themselves, mental problems will not arise again.

It is impossible to explain Buddhist psychotherapy without talking about meditation. In general, there are two kinds of meditation, the practice of seeing the body and mind macroscopically and microscopically. Seeing the body and mind macroscopically refers to the practice of observing the things that arise in the body and mind moment to moment. Through this practice, we can understand the body and

H. Jeon, *Buddhist Psychotherapy*, https://doi.org/10.1007/978-3-030-63098-0_6

mind well, develop wisdom, and improve our mental health. On the other hand, if we practice seeing microscopically, or practice Samatha and Vipassanā meditation, we will come to see our existence, or in other words the body and mind, as ultimate materiality and mentality. Through this we will come to know what kind of beings we are, how the body and mind is ultimately formed, and what kinds of phenomena arise in the body and mind from moment to moment.

In particular, if we practice Samatha and Vipassanā meditation, we will come to observe the cognitive process (see Chap. 1), and this experience will give us insight into our minds. There are at least hundred billion cognitive processes that occur within us each second. The cognitive processes that arise in this way are all connected with our karma. And when a mentality arises, a corresponding materiality also arises. The reason why our bodies feel heavy when we are in a bad mood is because the materiality that forms when we are upset is connected with the heaviness of the body.

When we have a mental illness, it means that a foundation was laid out that caused to inevitably arise. Under the same principle, if we want to be mentally healthy, we need to lay out a foundation that can allow us to get healthy. From the perspective of Buddhist psychotherapy, in order to lay out a solid foundation for good mental health, we must make it so that beneficial consciousnesses continue to arise.

Beneficial consciousnesses refer to those that are with wisdom and are without greed, hatred, and ignorance. Harmful consciousnesses are the opposite. When we see with our eyes, hear with our ears, smell with our nose, taste with our tongue, feel with our body, and deal with objects with our mind, if it is accompanied by greed, hatred, and ignorance and we cannot see the object as it is, it is a harmful consciousness. In other words, encountering an object and thinking, "this is permanent, this is satisfactory, and this is substantive" is unwise attention and a harmful consciousness. From the perspective of Samatha and Vipassanā meditation, encountering an object and thinking, "this is ultimate materiality, this is ultimate mentality, this is impermanent, this is unsatisfactory, this is not substantive, and this is impure" is wisdom and a beneficial consciousness.

Harmful consciousnesses and beneficial consciousnesses are connected with our karma. This means that when we have a harmful consciousness, that harm comes back to us, and when we have a beneficial consciousness, that benefit also comes back to us. Therefore, without even thinking about others, we need to make sure that we have good consciousnesses for our own sake. In that case, do we absolutely need some kind of extraordinary wisdom in order to make beneficial consciousnesses arise? No, we do not. Even just focusing on the present moment becomes a beneficial consciousness. If we think about the past while focusing on the present and we say, "the past is gone!" and return to the present, and if we think about the future and say, "the future is unknown!" and return to the present, this becomes a beneficial consciousness. When a thought about the past arises, if it leads to other thoughts such as "why did that person do this to me? And why did I do that?" it is becoming a harmful consciousness. Being in the present is the path to being free from greed, hatred, and ignorance. If we do this, we will always have beneficial consciousnesses, and our mental health will improve.

An arahant, the ideal for Buddhist practitioners, stays focused on the present throughout the entire day. If we continue to focus on the present, we too can get closer and closer to becoming an arahant. When I practiced Samatha and Vipassanā meditation, I first cultivated the absorptions (jhāna), then I practiced meditation on materiality. Meditation on materiality is the practice of seeing ultimate materiality. Materiality is formed in various ways, and one of those ways is through the mind. When we have a certain kind of consciousness, materiality is formed from it, which is something we can see when we practice meditation on materiality. We can see the materiality that is created from the mind when we make up our minds to do something. We are constantly making up our minds all day. Materiality forms as a result, and since we see that materiality when practicing meditation on materiality, it is impossible to not be focused on the present. The foundation is laid out to be able to focus all day. When this happens, we can automatically enter into a state of mindfulness.

However, it is difficult to practice Samatha meditation and meditation on materiality. In order to do this, we have to strive in our practice like a monk or nun, but since we as regular people have to make a living, it can be extremely difficult to create the conditions to be able to practice. However, even if we do not necessarily practice meditation, if we diligently read the Abhidhamma, cultivate faith by thinking, "as the Buddha has said, if we practice meditation we see things in this way. I will also see things in this way," and live according to it, you can also achieve this. Books such *Samatha, Jhāna, and Vipassanā* which I wrote and *The Essence of the Buddha's Abhidhamma* by Dr. Mehm Tin Mon can also be references for Samatha meditation and meditation on materiality.

Pharmaceutical Treatment

As I have said before, the most important thing for treatment is right effort. Just as the reason why a mental illness arises is because the person undergoes a process that led to it, in order to escape from it they need to exert the right effort. Therefore, the therapist must help the patient make the right effort. However, there are some patients who say that they are too anxious or depressed and are therefore in a state where they cannot make the right effort. For example, it is times when the thoughts that make the patient anxious and depressed arise one after another so much that their state only gets more and more worse, leaving them with no space. One thing that can be considered when this happens is pharmaceutical therapy. Taking medicine can help the patient stop having the thoughts that give them a hard time, and even if they have those thoughts, it can help them not to be as influenced by them. Once the anxiety and depression calm down by borrowing the power of medicine like this, space opens for the patient and the therapist to intervene and cultivate right effort.

Pharmaceutical therapy should also be considered in cases where it becomes difficult for the patient to go about living their lives due to the effects of physical symptoms. If the patient experiences symptoms such as difficulty of breathing or sudden increase in heart rate caused by mental problems, the therapist needs to calm the patient down by giving them medicine. This is also in order to solidify the foundation of being able to exert the right effort by stabilizing the patient's life.

When prescribing medicine, it is always necessary to sufficiently consult with the patient. Not only does the therapist need to provide accurate information about drugs to the patient, but they need to also reassure the patient of any repulsion towards medicine they may have. It is good if the therapist begins prescribing medicine once the patient expresses their intention to try it. The therapist must not thoughtlessly emphasize medicine without going through this kind of process. Also, even if the therapist and patient decide to use medicine, the focus should still remain on cultivating right effort. Medicine alone is limited. This is because if the conditions that led to the mental illness, such as the way the patient deals with difficult situations or their work environment, remain as they are, then the mental illness could arise again in the future. Therefore, we need to combine pharmaceutical therapy with right effort. During this process, once the patient improves through their effort, they can take less medicine until eventually they can stop taking it altogether. However, the therapist should avoid reducing the patient's medicine just because they want to reduce it or stop taking it. The problem may worsen to the extent that the medicine has been reduced.

There is something else that the patient and the therapist must be aware of regarding medicine and mental health. This may sound strange, but it is good to avoid looking at information about medicine or mental health as much as possible. Though I myself am also a doctor, when I have an orthopedic problem or I get sick, I immediately seek out the appropriate medical specialist. This is because I understand that I do not have the ability to make a judgment on my condition. In the same way, one thing I always request to my patients is to avoid searching for common health knowledge concerning mental health on the internet.

In the past one patient came to me and said that he was a schizophrenic, even though from my perspective he was suffering from neurosis. When I asked why he thought that way, he said that was what he found when he searched the internet. So I told him. "I've seen patients suffering from schizophrenia for over 30 years, and this isn't the case for you." If we make decisions based only on information about health, it is easy for us to believe that we have a certain kind of illness. This is because we do not have the skill to look at that information properly. Skill comes from experience on that particular field. Therefore, it is difficult for someone who does not have professional experience in the field of health to properly interpret information about health.

For example, there are many reasons why we may have problems with digestion. We could have eaten the wrong food, we may be tired, it may be because of a stomach infection or a stomach ulcer, or it may be because of stomach cancer. A doctor who specializes in internal medicine can determine the cause much more accurately as they have the experience of seeing patients for a long time. However, someone who does not have that skill may take fragmentary information and make the wrong decision, which could end up harming them. For example, they may think that what is just some indigestion and a little weight loss is stomach cancer, which will immediately make them fall into a state of anxiety.

I often go out of my way to tell patients not to look at information about medicine. Among the patients I prescribe medicine to, there are some who come back later and tell me they will not take it. I sometimes prescribe medicine for bipolar disorder to help patients deal with anger management, sometimes prescribe medicine for anxiety to those with depression, and sometimes prescribe medicine used to treat epilepsy to patients suffering from bipolar disorder. If I think they need it based on my experience, I will prescribe it. But there are times when the patient will read about the medicine and will distrust me and not take the medicine. This is likely because they are not able to fully understand all of the uses the medicine has.

In the case of psychosis, medicine must be the basis for its treatment. Schizophrenia, bipolar disorder, and paranoia are the three main kinds of psychosis, and in these cases, there has either been a disruption in the patient's neurotransmitter metabolism, or they are in a state where its balance has been completely broken. If they do not take medicine, they will not be able to see reality properly, which will make it hard to engage in dialog with them, and in extreme cases may even lead to an accident. Therefore, the patient needs to have medicine as the basis of treatment along with things such as psychotherapy and family therapy. It becomes necessary for not only the patient themselves, but also those around them to all work together to help the patient recover.

When treating psychosis with medicine, there are guidelines that psychiatrists follow. If it is the first time that the psychosis has arisen, we usually prescribe medicine until the symptoms disappear, and continue prescribing it for around 2 more years. However, in the case of relapse, we have the patient take medicine for around 5 years after the symptoms disappear though there may be exceptions to this. Methods such as Buddhist psychotherapy, when entered into the treatment of the patient, allow the patient to see their minds moment to moment and deal with them. This may help the patient be able to stop taking medicine earlier.

There are some cases where I recommend that the patient be admitted to a mental hospital. Usually, this happens in cases such as those that follow. First, in cases where they do not do their daily activities. There are some psychotic patients who will not do anything, including eating and washing themselves. It is good for those people to be admitted to a mental hospital so that they can embark on a process of restoring their daily activities by following a program at the hospital. Second, those who will not take medicine. As I have said before, because medicine is the foundation of treating psychosis, if the patient refuses to take medicine, it can be necessary to admit them into a mental hospital even by force. Third, cases where there is a danger of violence, self-harm, or suicide. Usually, these people are in a state of extreme suffering. If they are admitted into a mental hospital, it may help them calm down their minds to eliminate such impulses.

Meditation and Practice

Let us think about the effects meditation has on treatment. Just a few years ago, there were not many doctors who used meditation in their treatment. However, nowadays the effectiveness of meditation on treatment has become so widely known that an association where psychiatrists and doctors in general research meditation scientifically and medically has emerged in Korea, and meditation has become a part of treatment in places as large as university hospitals.

Meditation can be described in many ways, but in essence, meditation is focusing on the present moment. In other words, meditation is letting go when the mind has gone to a place that is not the present. Because it is the mind's function to always take a hold of a single object, it has no choice but to let other things go in order to focus on the present. There are several reasons why people go to meditation centers or seek out a quiet space when practicing meditation. One reason is because when we are at those kinds of places, there are not many conditions that turn our interest outward, making it easier for us to focus on the present. If we are able to focus on the present like this and completely let go of everything else, we will be able to enter absorption. In particular, if we enter the fourth absorption, only the mind's function of seeing will remain. Therefore, we will not be disturbed by things such as thoughts or emotions, and we will be able to clearly understand the object of meditation as it is.

When we talk about the first principle of Buddhist psychotherapy namely the properties of the body mind, we said that the mind becomes healthy when it goes to a wholesome object, and it becomes unhealthy when it goes to an unwholesome object. If we practice meditation diligently, we will establish a system of focusing and letting go within ourselves. As a result, it will become easier to focus on wholesome objects and let go of unwholesome objects. Even if there's something that puts us in a bad mood, we will be able to quickly shake it off. The mind will naturally become healthier. This is the first reason why meditation is effective for treatment.

In fact, the object itself is actually a neutral thing; it is neither wholesome nor unwholesome. It is just that if our attention towards that object is wise, it becomes a wholesome object, and if it is unwise, it becomes an unwholesome object. For example, when something from our past comes to mind and we give it wise attention thinking, "this is the past. It has already gone," at that moment a beneficial consciousness will arise, and the past will become a wholesome object. On the other hand, if thoughts such as regret, shame, and yearning arise following the past event, at that moment a harmful consciousness will arise, and the past will become an unwholesome object. The practice of meditation helps the mind to have wise attention towards objects. This is the second reason why meditation is effective for treatment.

In order to be mentally healthy, we have to have to get rid of the belief in self. Belief in self refers to perceiving things like, "my body, my mind, me." The method of getting rid of the belief in self is simple. If we continue to focus on and observe the body and mind from the moment we wake up in the morning to the moment we fall asleep at night, we will eventually come to know that the body and mind are not ours. We will realize that the body and mind changes according to their conditions, regardless of our own will. When we come to know this, we will no longer do things that harm the body and mind. This means no longer creating our own suffering. This is the third reason why meditation is effective for treatment.

Once there was a patient who came to me and said that he had an ear infection. He was extremely uncomfortable, worried, and anxious, and would constantly complain. Because he was anxious, he kept searching the internet, and based on that information, he was extremely worried about what would happen to him in the future. I told him this, "You should leave it at the ear hurting, don't add anything else onto that. I will show you how you can do this." And after telling him this, I prescribed medicine to help him with his current state. What accompanied this patient's ear infection was a mental problem.

Let us say that the same ear infection came up in a doctor who specializes in otolaryngology. Would the same mental problem as the one that arose in my patient also have arisen in that doctor? That doctor would likely only have experienced the ear pain. As an otolaryngologist, they would understand how the ear functions and would probably not have any unnecessary worries. Likewise, if we see and know well, we can stop creating suffering for ourselves. Additionally, if we practice meditation, we will come to see that it is obvious for us to experience the suffering that is inevitable in our existence, and we will come to accept it naturally. This kind of accepting attitude is also extremely important for our mental health.

In this way, if we practice meditation we will be able to observe ourselves well. In Western psychoanalysis, there are two egos, the experiencing ego, and the observing ego. Here the experiencing ego performs actions while the observing ego observes the self that performs those actions. If we are angry, the experiencing ego only performs the function of getting angry. The observing ego will observe this situation and will function to try and control that anger. The observing ego will tell us, "if I continue to get angry like this, it'll be harmful, so I should stop." In another example, it is the function of the observing ego that separates the "R" sound from the "L" sound and corrects our pronunciation when speaking English. In psychoanalysis, treatment is divided into the early, middle, and late stages, and when the patient's observing ego functions properly, they will progress from the early to the middle stage of treatment. When the power of observation increases through meditation, we can say that the observing ego becomes stronger. This means that even when we look at it from the perspective of psychoanalysis, meditation has a positive effect on our mental health.

Therefore, in order to be mentally healthy, we need to establish the roots of meditation in our lives. The practice of meditation doing its job means that the way we live our lives becomes meditation and practice. Though there is still a need to set aside the time and space to practice sitting or walking meditation, it is important to observe the experiences of our daily lives as if we are meditating. Thinking that we can do whatever we want with the rest of our time because we are practicing meditation for an hour once a day is not a very good attitude. We must make it so that formal meditation and observation within our lives always comes together.

Sleeping Well

Sleep takes up a significant portion of our lives. Though it depends on the person, we usually spend a third of our lives sleeping. However, there is no shortage of people who suffer from not being able to sleep well. Among the people who seek me out are those who have a hard time due to insomnia. For these patients, I show them a technique I learned to sleep well.

The heart does not beat according to our will, but does so autonomously. Sleep is the same way. Sleep is a system that functions through the autonomic nervous system. The autonomic nervous system is affected by sympathetic nerves and parasympathetic nerves. The stimulation or activation of sympathetic nerves hinders our sleep, while the stimulation or activation of parasympathetic nerves helps our sleep. Sympathetic nerves indicate the mind exerting effort. When we have trouble falling asleep, we usually think, "I need to sleep. I'll be in big trouble if I can't sleep. Tomorrow will be ruined if I can't sleep," worrying and exerting a lot of effort to try and sleep. What happens then? Sympathetic nerves become activated and we are not able to sleep well. Parasympathetic nerves are when the mind lets go and just goes according to nature. It is accepting, "If I fall asleep, then I'll asleep. If I don't fall asleep, I can just close my eyes and rest."

If we look at it physiologically, it is good to sleep at 11 o'clock or 12 o'clock at the latest and wake up at around 7 o'clock in the morning. Because sleep is a kind of biological clock, it is good to lay down when the time comes, whether or not we are fall asleep. It is also important to get rid of light by turning everything off. This is because darkness stimulates the sleep center of the human body, while light stimulates the awake center. Also, it is good to have the following mindset when laying down, "How wonderful is it that I can lay down like this at the end of the day!" The next stage is to activate the parasympathetic nerves. We can do this by adopting the following mindset, "Now, there is only one thing to do from this moment until I wake up the next day: sleeping if I fall asleep and resting if I don't." It is actually quite simple. We sleep if we can, and if we cannot, we lay down with our eyes closed and rest, thinking "it looks like I don't need to sleep right now. But I should rest now."

Though it is simple in principle, usually the reason why people struggle with this is because of thoughts. If we just lay still, thoughts will usually start coming one after another. We need to deal with these thoughts well. We cannot do anything about the thoughts that arise. They arise because the conditions have been met for them to arise. Do not follow these thoughts. Rather than deliberating in your head about why thoughts arise, simply stop by thinking, "it seems like thoughts are arising because I'm not falling asleep." If thoughts arise again, just think, "They arose again," and once again stop. Since in many cases thinking causes us to stay awake, it is important to stop thoughts.

When we cannot fall asleep, it is difficult to lay down on straight on our backs. It can feel uncomfortable. When this happens, it is good to lay down while shifting from left to right. There is no need to be stubborn and force yourself thinking, "I have to sleep straight on my back." When we have trouble sleeping and feel uncomfortable, some people watch TV or look at their smartphones. You must not do this. If a stimulus enters our eyes, it becomes harder to fall asleep. Also, do not leave your bed just because you are having trouble falling asleep. Rather, it is good to keep laying down, close your eyes, and focus on the breath. Electroencephalography tests have shown that when we focus on the breath, we enter a state of being half asleep. This allows us to fall asleep without even realizing it. If you are feeling too uncomfortable because you are struggling to sleep, it is also good to sit up with your eyes closed and focus on the breath for a bit before laying down again. You should not get up and move about however. This makes people very exhausted. Of course, this does not mean that you should not get up to go to the bathroom. The sleep we need will come, so just relax the mind.

If fall asleep when you can or spend the night relaxing the mind and resting when you cannot, you will not be very tired. In my clinical experience, there were generally two things that happened in cases where people were exhausted from not being able to sleep. One was the case where they went around and did things because they was not falling asleep, and the other was the case where they did not move about but exerted a lot of effort to try and sleep. If you relax your mind in the way I explained, you will not be very exhausted. Try it and you will know.

Additionally, doing a body scan can help a lot in falling asleep. I found that prescribing body scanning to patients who suffer from insomnia has been quite effective. Body scanning means closing your eyes and scanning your entire body. I usually start from my toes. First, I just try to feel the big toe on my left foot. I do this by just placing my attention on the big toe of my left foot while letting go of the will to try to feel it well. After feeling out my toes one by one like this, I try to feel all of my toes. Afterwards, I imagine that the breath enters and leaves through the toes. I imagine the breath entering the toes, staying there, and leaving. If my toes are uncomfortable, I imagine that the discomfort leaves as my breath goes out. In this way, I feel my toes getting more comfortable.

After doing this, I then turn my attention to the top of my left foot. I first try to feel the skin, and then I try to feel the muscles, vessels, and nerves underneath the skin. Then, I imagine that the breath enters the top of my foot, stays there, and leaves. As I did for my toes, if the top of my foot is uncomfortable, I imagine that the discomfort leaves as my breath goes out and I feel the top of my foot getting more comfortable. I follow the same process for my left ankle, shin, calf, knee, all the way up to the left thigh. Once I go through my entire left leg from the toes to the thigh, I do the same with the right leg from the toes to the thigh. After I have finished scanning both feet and both legs, I turn my attention to the pelvis, stomach, chest, waist, back, shoulders, arms, hands, neck, the parts of my face, the scalp, and to the crown of my head and go through the same process. At the very end, I imagine that the breath which enters the crown of my head goes through the entire body and leaves through the toes, and the breath which enters the toes goes through the entire body and leaves through the crown of my head. When the breath leaves, I imagine that the discomfort in my body leaves with it, and I feel the body getting more comfortable.

When doing a body scan like this, it is important to let go of the goal of falling asleep. Since we cannot fall asleep anyways, we have nothing else to do, and we are tired, it is good to make up our minds to just rest comfortably while scanning our bodies. I have never gotten past the ankle when doing body scans while laying down in bed. I am very sensitive to caffeine and so I have trouble falling asleep when I drink coffee. But when I tried body scanning after drinking coffee, even that sensitivity dulled to some extent. Though I was still unable to fall asleep, I noticed a clear difference. It is good to not just do body scanning when we sleep but also to do it in our spare time. For example, if your shoulders feel heavy and uncomfortable, do a body scan on the shoulder area. Then the discomfort will ease, and you will feel more relaxed.

I will end by talking about an experience I had that may help lessen the anxiety around not being able to fall asleep. Once when I went to India in 2009 to meet the Dalai Lama, I had an incredibly hard time with a rash that went over my entire body. I was not able to find a dermatologist, and so I endured it for about a month and went to the hospital after coming back to Korea. When I went to the dermatologist, they prescribed me with a lot of steroids. I took shots and medicine. I took steroids and an antihistamine for about 3 weeks and continued taking antihistamines for 9 months afterwards. Once I stopped taking medicine, I was completely unable to fall asleep. So, because I was not able to sleep what all, I did the things that I have been discussing up to this point: I laid still and focused on my breath all night. When I woke up in the morning, it was manageable. After spending a week like this without being able to fall asleep, I naturally fell asleep on the eighth day. From this experience, I learned that even if you do not actually fall asleep, if you lay down with a relaxed mind, you will not really have any problems.

Psychiatrist Victor Frankle pointed out in his book *Man's Search for Meaning* that "the fear of sleeplessness results in a hyper-intention to fall asleep, which, in turn, incapacitates the patient to do so" [1]. He says that organisms will find a way to get their bare minimum requirement of sleep on their own, and recommends to patients who have anxiety about insomnia to not try to sleep but to try and stay awake as long as possible. Paradoxically, they will then be able to fall asleep immediately.

Dealing with Pain in the Body and Mind

During the summer of 2003, I spent a month as a monk in the Chanmyay Meditation Center. The meditation we practiced there was observing all the phenomena that arose. It was summer time and I was constantly being bit by mosquitoes. They would bite me while I sat and while I walked. But I was not able to kill them. This is because a monk has to follow 227 monastic rules, and among them is a rule that you cannot kill living beings. Also, since a practitioner had to always observe the phenomena that arose, I was not able to chase the mosquitoes away either. And so for the first time in my life, I fully observed a mosquito land on my arm, suck its fill of blood, and fly away.

When a mosquito bites you, the itchiness does not begin right away. Rather, there is a delay. When mosquitoes in Myanmar bit me, it would at first be much itchier than those in Korea, but afterwards that itchiness completely disappeared. As I continued to observe, the degree of itchiness decreased significantly. It was manageable. Before when a mosquito bit me, the degree of itchiness would be a 10, whereas when I observed the sensation without any intentions to scratch it, it would be about a 3. This happened even though I was not even trying to get rid of the itchiness and rather just observed it. Curious about the reason why the degree of itchiness decreased, I thought about it for some time and came up on my own with three mechanisms. If you keep this in mind, it will help you understand and deal with pain in the body.

First, when we feel itchy, we have an emotional reaction. Why is it itchy, what do we do it if itches again, etc. It seems like these emotional reactions amplify the itchiness. When you just observe it, there is no emotional reaction and so the itchiness does not amplify, and you only feel the itchiness that is actually there. This is why it is less itchy.

Second, as you observe the itchiness, it sometimes appears and sometimes disappears. You are not continuously itchy. Itchiness occurs when some substance is secreted, and when this does not happen, the itchiness is not there. When I felt the absence of itchiness like this, it seemed to lessen the overall itchiness.

Third, observing the entire process means coming to know the changes that occur in itchiness. Since I observed when the itchiness was absent, when it started to be itchy, when the itchiness reached its peak, and when it eventually disappeared completely, I was able to be more composed towards itchiness.

I have athlete's foot and so from time to time I have to take care of my toenails. When the toenail sticks to the skin and I have to remove it, it is extremely painful. Once, I tried just observing that pain just like I had observed itchiness. When I did this, just like in the case of itchiness, the pain also decreased significantly. Observing was also useful for managing pain. And from then on, I was no longer afraid of pain. Once I ran a "8 Week Meditation and Self-Healing" program over a year and a half. During that time, one person who attended the program had a similar experience. Before participating in the program, he hated going to the dentist more than anything, but after practicing meditation during that program, he was able to be relaxed when he went to the dentist. This was thanks to the power of observing.

And one more thing. This is a tip, but hospitals will not conduct painful treatments that are hard for patients to cope with. This is because a patient will go into shock if that kind of pain occurs. And so I trust the surgeons thinking, "that person won't give me pain that is hard for me to cope with." Having this kind of trust helps put your anxiety to rest and helps you relax.

Observing not only helps us deal with pain in the body, but also suffering in the mind. Suffering in the mind refers to discomfort in the mind due to things like anger, doubt, and anxiety. Once when my mind became uncomfortable, I tried observing this uncomfortable mind. I observed the uncomfortable mind just as I had observed itchiness. Usually, I try to think of this and that to bring my mind to ease, but this time I did not do that and just observed the mind as it was. When I did that, the anxious mind disappeared like the wind parting away clouds that gathered around a mountain. The principle for this is as follows: the mind always goes towards some object and is affected by it. The reason why the mind was uncomfortable is because the mind went to an object that makes it uncomfortable and was affected by it. But our attention moved away from the object that made our minds uncomfortable and went to the object of being aware of the phenomena that arose. Then, it is inevitable that the discomfort in the mind would disappear.

While I was not able to avoid the pain that comes with having a body and mind, through these experiences I came to be certain that we can reduce or get rid of pain that we create.

Escaping from Obsessive-Compulsive Disorder

Obsessive-compulsive disorder can be explained from two perspectives. One is the perspective of brain science and the other is based on an understanding of the properties of the mind. Let us first look at obsessive-compulsive disorder from the perspective of brain science. My explanation from the perspective of brain science will be based on the book *Brain Lock: Free Yourself from Obsessive-Compulsive Behavior* by UCLA psychiatrist Jeffrey M. Schwartz. I recommend reading the book if you want to know about it in more detail.

The areas of the brain associated with obsessive-compulsive disorder are the caudate nucleus, putamen, orbital cortex, and the cingulate gyrus. The caudate nucleus is a system that changes the way we think while the putamen is a system that changes the way we act. For example, let us say that after seeing dirty hands, a message came down from the front of our brains (the frontal lobe) down to the caudate nucleus to wash our hands. Then, the putamen connected to the caudate nucleus will change gears to "wash our hands," after which we wash our hands. Here, someone with a normal caudate nucleus will change their thinking once they have washed their hands. On the other hand, someone with obsessive-compulsive disorder will not experience this change in thought and their caudate nucleus will be stuck with the message to wash their hands. The gears of the putamen will likewise be stuck with washing their hands. This is why they keep washing their hands.

The caudate nucleus is also associated with the orbital cortex. The orbital cortex searches for erroneous information. A normal person will be able to discern the existence of erroneous information from their orbital cortex, but this does not work well for someone who has problems in their orbital cortex. When you have washed your hands and they are clean, the orbital cortex needs to discern from the hands that the error has been eliminated and should stop the acting, but someone who has problems with their orbital cortex will continue to receive the message that there is an error (dirtiness) in their hands. This message gets repeatedly sent to the caudate nucleus, which causes them to wash their hands repeatedly.

Finally, when something is not done, a feeling that something terrible will happen arises from cingulate gyrus. In the case of a person who has the compulsion to keep washing their hands, an anxiety that something terrible will happen arises from their cingulate gyrus, and they will keep washing their hands in order to resolve this anxiety.

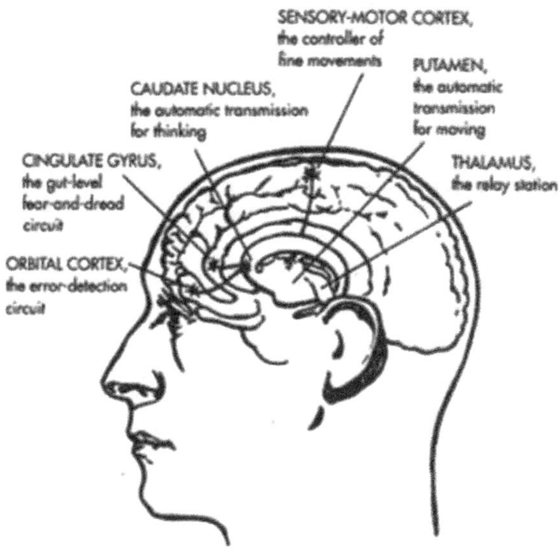

Jeffrey Schwartz's research team recommends action-based treatment through right effort to patients suffering from obsessive-compulsive disorder rather than pharmaceutical therapy. This is because the treatment effects of pharmaceutical therapy and action-based treatment are similar. Of course, they combine pharmaceutical therapy in cases where it is necessary. During treatment, this team uses functional magnetic resonance images (fMRI). They take an image when the patient first comes, take another image after they have helped the patient make the right effort, and show the patient the changes between those two images. If you look at the images of the patient's initial state, the parts associated with obsessive-compulsive disorder are brightly activated, but in the images after the patient has made the right effort, the decrease in the activation levels of those areas really stands out. Patients who have confirmed a distinct change in the images of their own brain will begin to believe in the effects of right effort and will make even more of an effort, eventually allowing them to escape from obsessive-compulsive disorder entirely.

This team prescribes the "15-minute method" to patients. For example, when the impulse to wash their hand arises, the patient is to ignore that impulse for 15 min and do something else. Patients have already seen the effects of the 15-minute method from fMRI images. Therefore, they will come to accept impulses to action like this, “This is erroneous information. If I follow it, the symptoms will become more and more worse. I’ve seen through images that things will get better if I restrain myself now, so I’ll restrain myself even though it’s hard.” However, it is extremely difficult to restrain oneself in this case. This is because signals of something terrible happening like the gas tank exploding in your house, a burglar coming into an open door, or contracting a disease from your hands being infected by germs will continuously come out from the cingulate gyrus. But if just 15 or so minutes pass, those impulses will usually subside. If they do not subside, you should then continue to make an effort to restrain yourself in 15-minute increments. Then those impulses of compulsive behavior will eventually subside. If this effort is maintained constantly, a new pathway will open up in the brain and it will become easier to make the right effort. Gradually, the brain will change, and you will escape from obsessive-compulsive disorder.

Now let us look at obsessive-compulsive disorder on the basis of understanding the mind’s properties. I have said many times before that the property of the mind is to always go towards an object, thereby being affected by it. If we look at people who are experiencing symptoms of obsessive-compulsive disorder, they usually have the beginning stage of the symptoms. At this beginning stage, something will cause them anxiety and make them uncomfortable, and they will come to keep thinking those things. So the pathways of their minds that point towards those objects will have been opened wide.

In order to feel at ease, someone suffering from obsessive-compulsive disorder will think of resolving that state of anxiety. However, those thoughts are not separate from the state of anxiety but rather connected to it. Regardless of what someone who has the compulsion to keep washing their hands thinks, those thoughts will still inevitably be connected with the compulsion to keep washing their hands. What could this mean? I will explain it through the example of poisonous gas. Let us imagine that poisonous gas has leaked into this place right now. What should we do? We need to quickly move to a place where there is no poisonous gas. But someone who suffers from obsessive-compulsive disorder will act in way of looking for a place within the poisonous gas where it is slightly less concentrated. However, no matter how much they do this, they will not be able to avoid being harmed by the poisonous gas.

When we look at it from the perspective of the mind’s properties, in order to cut ourselves off from obsessive-compulsive disorder, we need to stop the thoughts that are related to obsessive-compulsive disorder. To do this, we need to train ourselves to let go of thoughts. One patient who suffered from obsessive compulsive disorder that I treated was really dedicated to the practice of letting go of thoughts. He suffered from an extremely severe case of obsessive-compulsive disorder, but was eventually able to escape from it through this practice. Obsessive-compulsive thoughts are extremely difficult thought to break free from. If our ability to let go of thoughts is not strong enough, it is like a trap that is hard to escape from. Therefore, we need to strengthen our ability to let go of thoughts by consistently practicing things like focusing on the present in our daily lives.

The Buddha said the following about letting go of thoughts in "The Discourse on the Removal of Distracting Thoughts" in the Majjhima Nikāya (MN 20). I will not quote the entire discourse but present an abridged version.

The Discourse on the Removal of Distracting Thoughts

> "Bhikkhus, when a bhikkhu is pursuing the higher mind, from time to time he should give attention to five signs. What are the five?"
>
> "Here, bhikkhus, when a bhikkhu is giving attention to some sign, and owing to that sign there arise in him evil unwholesome thoughts connected with desire, with hate, and with delusion, then (1) he should give attention to some other sign connected with what is wholesome... Just as a skilled carpenter or his apprentice might knock out, remove, and extract a coarse peg by means of a fine one. (2) If, while he is giving attention to some other sign connected with what is wholesome, there still arises in him evil unwholesome thoughts connected with desire, with hate, and with delusion, then he should examine the danger in those thoughts thus: 'These thoughts are unwholesome, they are reprehensible, they result in suffering.' ... Just as a man or a woman, young, youthful, and fond of ornaments, would be horrified, humiliated, and disgusted if the carcass of a snake or a dog or a human being were hung around his or her neck. (3) If, while he is examining the danger in those thoughts, there still arises in him evil unwholesome thoughts connected with desire, with hate, and with delusion, then he should try to forget those thoughts and should not give attention to them... Just as a man with good eyes who did not want to see forms that had come within range of sight would either shut his eyes or look away. (4) If, while he is trying to forget these thoughts and is not giving attention to them, there still arises in him evil unwholesome thoughts connected with desire, with hate, and with delusion, then he should give attention to stilling the thought-formation of those thoughts... Just as a man walking fast might consider: 'Why am I walking fast? What if I walk slowly?' and he would walk slowly; then he might consider: 'Why am I walking slowly? What if I stand?' and he would stand; then he might consider: 'Why am I standing? What if I sit?' and he would sit; then he might consider: 'Why am I sitting? What if I lie down?' and he would lie down. By doing so he would substitute for each grosser posture one that was subtler. (5) If, while he is giving attention to stilling the thought-formation of those thoughts, there still arises in him evil unwholesome thoughts connected with desire, with hate, and with delusion, then, with his teeth clenched and his tongue pressed against the roof of his mouth, he should beat down, constrain, and crush [unwholesome] mind with [wholesome] mind... Just as a strong man might seize a weaker man by the head or shoulders and beat him down, constrain him, and crush him."
>
> "Bhikkhus, when a bhikkhu does this any evil unwholesome thoughts connected with desire, with hate, and with delusion are abandoned in him and subside, and with the abandoning of them his mind becomes steadied internally, quieted, brought to singleness, and concentrated... This bhikkhu is then called a master of the courses of thought. He will think whatever thought he wishes to think and he will not think any thought that he does not wish to think. He has severed craving, flung off the fetters, and with the complete penetration of conceit he has made an end to suffering". [2]

Though these are words that the Buddha spoke to those who were practicing Samatha meditation, they can also be applied to our own daily lives. We can make a kind of "five-step manual for practicing letting go of thoughts," and apply this step by step when a difficult situation arises.

For example, let us imagine there is a situation where we come across someone who has harmed us greatly in the past, causing us to get angry. Here, the first step that we can take is to bring to mind a wholesome object. We can bring to mind someone who we are thankful for that has helped us in the past. If we bring to mind this person who we are thankful for, warmth will spread through our minds and diffuse our tension. Though it is not easy to do this since we are angry, if we make this a manual and apply it from time to time as necessary, it will become possible.

If we have moved our minds to a wholesome object but our anger has still not calmed down, we can go onto the second stage. This is thinking of the fact that thoughts that arouse anger will harm ourselves. When we think of thoughts that arouse anger, our mind will actually become unstable and our body will also not be in a good state. Also, we will become distracted and will not be able to do the things that we actually need to do. It is clearly harmful. Therefore, we will let go of that unwholesome thought by contemplating, "this is my loss. It causes me harm and doesn't help me at all."

If this still does not work, we go onto the third stage. This is preventing the mind from even going to an unwholesome object. Here, we can use the method that some Western teachers of meditation use, namely to "anchor" our minds. This means setting up an object of concentration that is normally easy for us to use such as our breath or the feeling of the sole of our feet and turning our attention to that object.

If the unwholesome thoughts still persist, we move onto the fourth stage and make an effort to calm the cause of those thoughts. If we look at it from a Buddhist perspective, the reason why we have unwholesome thoughts is due to the greed, hatred, and ignorance within us. Therefore, we will look at what kind of greed, hatred, and delusion is inside of us and will let it go. This was expressed in the following way in the discourse: "Just as a man walking fast might consider: 'Why am I walking fast? What if I walk slowly?' and he would walk slowly; then he might consider: 'Why am I walking slowly? What if I stand?' and he would stand; then he might consider: 'Why am I standing? What if I sit?' and he would sit; then he might consider: 'Why am I sitting? What if I lie down?' and he would lie down. By doing so he would substitute for each grosser posture one that was subtler." In this way, we can contemplate the roots of our unwholesome thoughts and little by little escape from their influence.

If it still does not work after the fourth stage, we will move onto the fifth stage. This is suppressing the unwholesome thought by gritting our teeth and thinking of it as a life-and-death situation.

When I introduced the passage from this discourse to one patient suffering from obsessive compulsive disorder and explained its meaning and method of application, he made into a manual, wrote it down in his notebook, always kept it with him, read it and appreciated its meaning from time to time. He said that it was a great help to him. I also encourage all of you to make your own manual.

Final Words

This concludes my lectures on Buddhist Psychotherapy. Thank you all for taking the time to listen. I will say this again, but this is just the beginning. In order to change our lives through Buddhist psychotherapy, we must all study Buddhism and practice mediation, and apply these things to our own lives.

I consider reading Buddhist scriptures to be the core to studying Buddhism. This is because no matter what anyone says, the teacher of Buddhism has always been the Buddha, and the scriptures are records of what the Buddha said. We need to learn through the scriptures how the Buddha understood and solved the suffering of human beings. And I also recommend studying Buddhist scriptures with a group rather than just doing it on your own. It is good if you take what you have learned from the scriptures and experience it directly for yourselves through meditation. If you practice meditation, your understanding will deepen and become clearer, and through that process your own problems will also be resolved. When this happens, you will come to live a life that is not only good for yourself but will also have a good impact on those around you.

I hope you all make a lot of progress in the future.

References

1. Frankel V (1959) Man's search for meaning. Beacon Press, Boston, MA, p 150
2. Bodhi B (trans) (1995) The middle length discourses of the Buddha: a translation of the Majjhima Nikāya. Wisdom Publications, Somerville, pp 211–214

Index

H. Jeon, *Buddhist Psychotherapy*, https://doi.org/10.1007/978-3-030-63098-0

The manufacturer's authorised representative in the EU is Springer Nature Customer Service Centre GmbH, Europaplatz 3, 69115 Heidelberg, Germany. If you have any concerns regarding our products, please contact ProductSafety@springernature.com

Printed and bound by CPI Group (UK) Ltd, Croydon, CR0 4YY
28/09/2026
02224070-0019